ANTICHRIST *and the* END TIMES

ISBN: 1-891903-34-9

Distributed by:
St. Andrew's Productions
6091 Steubenville Pike, Bldg. 1, Unit #7
McKees Rocks, PA 15136

Tel: 412-787-9735
Fax: 412-787-5024
Web: www.SaintAndrew.com

Cover illustration: Luca Signorelli's depiction of Antichrist's demonic twin (1441-1523)

Printed in the United States of America

ANTICHRIST
and the
END TIMES

Rev. Joseph L. Iannuzzi

St. Andrew's Productions
McKees Rocks, PA

TABLE OF CONTENTS

CHAPTER 1

ANTICHRIST

In Sacred Scripture Jesus presents himself as the Good Shepherd who goes in search of the lost sheep.[1] The image of the Good Shepherd is a consoling image of a God that is here to save us, especially those that go astray. It is an image that is discovered anew in the writings of the early centuries of Christianity. Early Christianity includes the writings of the Apostles and of their followers, who are the early Church Fathers, Writers and Doctors. These early Christian writings develop the teachings of Christ. And they remind us that the God whose anger lasts a moment but whose mercy endures a thousand generations responds to anyone's appeal for mercy. In recent years Jesus revealed to the 20th century Polish mystic St. Faustina Kowlaska (1905-1938) that in preparing the world for his coming,[2] he does no want to punish mankind but to save it:

> In the Old Covenant I sent prophets wielding thunderbolts to My people. Today I am sending you with My mercy to the people of the whole world. I do not want to punish mankind, but I desire to heal it, pressing it to My Merciful Heart. I use punishment when they themselves force Me to do so; My hand is reluctant to take hold of the sword of justice. Before the Day of Justice, I am sending the Day of Mercy.[3]

---

[1] Jn. 10:1, *New American Bible, St. Joseph Edition* (NY: Catholic Book Pub. Co, 1991).

[2] Those who have been authorized to promote the writings of St. Faustina Maria Kowlaska have stated that when Jesus speaks to her of an "imminent return" or "second coming," it does not refer to the end of the world, but to *the beginning of a new era in the life of the Church*.

[3] St. Maria Faustina, *Diary, Divine Mercy in My Soul* (Stockbridge, MA: Marians of the Immaculate Conception, 2000), entry 1588.

If God's merciful grace withholds the sword of justice, humanity's sins force his hand to chastise and correct it for its own betterment. God's merciful grace and humankind's sins are a theme quite familiar to eschatology. Eschatology explores grace and sin through the events of death and judgment, and the consequences of heaven, hell and purgatory. Anyone who applies himself to the study of eschatology soon finds himself face to face with the opposing forces of good and evil: God and Satan, Christ and Antichrist. It is precisely this figure of Antichrist that I intend to explore in this book.

Antichrist occupies part of the theological landscape in Sacred Scripture and in early Tradition. In Sacred Scripture Antichrist cannot be restricted to any one individual, but applies to *many evil individuals* throughout the course of history. However, early Tradition presents Antichrist more specifically as an evil individual in the days preceding our Lord's return. In Sacred Scripture one discovers that St. John is the only biblical writer to refer to "Antichrist" as any spirit that opposes God. Yet Antichrist assumes a more individualistic appearance in the Church's early Tradition. Since this early Tradition includes not only the writings of the Apostles, but also the writings of the early Church Fathers, Writers and Doctors that faithfully transmitted to us the teachings of the Apostles, it is considered a source of revelation no less reliable than Sacred Scripture. Indeed, early Christian literature presents Antichrist as an evil "individual" whose public debut signals the end times. In eschatology, one must realize that the expression "end times" is not the end of the world, but a continuum of historic events leading up to the world's consummation and the end of human history.

CHAPTER 2

MANY ANTICHRISTS

Admittedly, the many contradictions in Christian circles reveal the perplexities involved in attempting to discover Antichrist's true identity. Such a discovery is attainable only with research and study of the inspired sources of the Christian faith which include Sacred Scripture and Tradition. The more one probes these sources, the more one encounters greater explication of the chief end time protagonists, two of whom merit special attention—Jesus Christ and Antichrist.

Jesus Christ stands at the forefront of salvation history. He is the God-man, sent by the Father of lights, who assumed our human nature to redeem the human race and all creation from its slavery to sin and corruption. Conversely, Antichrist appears as the leader of a great apostasy. He is the diabolic man, sent by Satan, the father of lies to use a human nature to destroy the human race and all creation.

Today there are literally hundreds of self-styled prophets claiming to disclose Antichrist's true identity. To the bewilderment of the reader, many provide little, if any, historic data for a fair and balanced assessment. Despite St. Peter's exhortation to shun all personal, subjective methods of biblical interpretation in early Tradition, the market seems to be flooded with them. Anyone who has studied the hermeneutic principles of Scripture soon learns that the principal cause of God's inspired Word (the Holy Spirit) communicates through his instrumental cause (the inspired writer) within the parameters of his particular character, vocabulary, circumstances, age and limitations.[4] Without this background data, one

---

4   Pope Pius XII. "Divino Afflante Spiritu," 33-34, http://www.vatican.va/holy_
     father/pius_xii/encyclicals/index.htm: "The inspired writer is the living and
     reasonable instrument of the Holy Spirit... who uses his faculties and powers...

cannot possibly grasp the intended meaning of the inspired writer who reveals the person of Antichrist.

This notwithstanding, subjective interpretations of the Bible and early Church documents approached its zenith at the dawn of the last century when "Antichrist labeling" became increasingly fashionable. Personages like Adolph Hitler, Aleister Crowley, Saddam Hussein and others became suspicious candidates. Soon enough Antichrist was popularly known as any notoriously evil individual who arises in the 20th century. Following the more objective standard, one finds that St. John refers to Antichrist not only as an "individual," but also as a collectivity of history's evil protagonists, otherwise known as the "spirit of antichrist":

> Just as you heard that the antichrist was coming, so now many antichrists have appeared... Whoever denies the Father and the Son, this is the antichrist... Every spirit that does not acknowledge Jesus does not belong to God. This is the spirit of antichrist that, as you have heard, is to come, but in fact is already in the world.[5]

> Many deceivers have gone out into the world, those who do not acknowledge Jesus Christ as coming in the flesh; such is the deceitful one and the antichrist.[6]

Let the interpreter then, with all care and without neglecting any light derived from recent research, endeavor to determine the peculiar character and circumstances of the sacred writer, the age in which he lived, the sources written or oral to which he had recourse and the forms of expression he employed. Thus can he better understand who was the inspired author, and what he wishes to express by his writings."

[5] *New American Bible, St. Joseph Edition* (NY: Catholic Book Pub. Co, 1991) 1 Jn.2:18.22; 4:3.

[6] 2 Jn 7.

The beast... existed once... and yet it will come again.[7]

Cardinal Joseph Ratzinger (Pope Benedict XVI) comments on the many manifestations of the Antichrist:

> As far as the antichrist is concerned, we have seen that in the New Testament he always assumes the lineaments of contemporary history. *He cannot be restricted to any single individual. One and the same he wears many masks in each generation.*[8]

St. John qualifies the "spirit of antichrist" with those who "deny the Father and the Son," and as those "spirits that do not acknowledge Jesus." Manifestly, the many spirits that have denied the Father and the Son were, to some extent, antichristian precursors of the *one* whom St. John believes "is to come," or whom we have heard "was coming," and "will come again." That this individual Antichrist will come again is indicated in the Book of Revelation, where one encounters the "False Prophet" and "Gog" who will arise in the days preceding our Lord's return.

---

[7] Ez 36:27: "I will give you a new heart and place *a new Spirit within you*, taking from your body your stony hearts and giving you natural hearts. I will put *my Spirit within you* and make you live by my statutes, careful to observe my decrees."

[8] Johann Auer and Joseph Ratzinger, *Dogmatic Theology, Eschatology 9*, Catholic University of America Press, 1988, pp.199-200.

CHAPTER 3

INDIVIDUAL ANTICHRIST

Unlike the Preterists who relegate prophecy and its eschatological protagonists to the past, the Tradition of the Apostles, faithfully transmitted by the early Church Fathers and developed through the centuries, envisions two future manifestations of "the spirit of antichrist," which St. John calls the "False Prophet" who receives his authority from the beast, and "Gog" who receives his authority from Magog. If St. John is the only biblical author to use the term "Antichrist,"[9] others have made reference to it. St. Paul refers to a single eschatological Antichrist, or individual incarnation of the "spirit of Antichrist," preceding Our Lord's return:

> The day of the Lord is at hand. Let no one
> deceive you in any way. For unless the apostasy
> comes first and the lawless one is revealed, the
> one doomed to perdition, who opposes and exalts
> himself above every so-called god and object of
> worship, so as to seat himself in the temple of
> God, claiming that he is a god... whom the Lord
> [Jesus] will kill with the breath of his mouth and
> render powerless by the manifestation of his
> coming.[10]

We encounter similar references in the Books of Daniel, Ezekiel, Revelation, Matthew and Mark. Matthew and Mark place this antichristian individual in the third person singular, thereby recalling

---

[9]   1 Jn 2:18.22; 4:3.

[10]   2 Thes 2:2-4.8.

Paul's reference of a satanic man. Indeed, Mark's use of a masculine participle "standing" (*hestekota*) in the neuter noun suggests this. A careful study of Scripture reveals that Matthew, Mark and Paul present the same characteristics that define the Antichrist of the early Fathers, who arises in the end times to profane God's sanctuary, and to persecute and kill Christians. Paul's aforementioned description of Antichrist offers an additional piece of evidence: It appears to match the descriptions of the last individual Antichrist represented in the figure of Gog, who arises shortly before the end of the Era of Peace, and whom Jesus kills with the breath of his mouth.

3.1   Church Fathers

Daniel, Matthew, Mark and Paul speak of an individual "abomination of desolation," and the Fathers bolster this teaching in their descriptions of a certain "man." Since early patristic documents are as replete as Sacred Scripture with accounts of an individual male Antichrist, I limit myself to few notable extracts:

The early Church Father St. Irenaeus (140-202 A.D.) writes:

> Of the events which shall occur in the time of Antichrist is it shown that he, being an apostate and a robber, is anxious to be adored as God; and that, although a mere slave, he wishes himself to be proclaimed as a king. For he (Antichrist) being endued with all the power of the devil, shall come, not as a righteous king… but an impious, unjust, and lawless one; as an apostate, iniquitous and murderous; as a robber, concentrating in himself all satanic apostasy, and setting aside idols to persuade men that he himself is God, raising up himself as the only idol… of whom the apostle thus speaks in the second Epistle to the Thessalonians: "Unless there shall come a falling away first, and *the man of sin shall be revealed, the*

son of perdition, who opposeth and exalteth himself
above all that is called God."

Moreover, he, the apostle, also pointed this out...
"But when ye shall see the abomination of desolation,
which was spoken of by Daniel the prophet, standing
in the holy place (let him that readeth understand),
then let those who are in Judea flee to the
mountains; and he who is upon the house-top, let
him not come down to take anything out of his
house: for there shall then be great hardship, such
as has not been from the beginning of the world
until now, nor ever shall be."

Daniel too, looking forward to the last kingdom,
i.e., the ten last kings... and upon whom the son
of perdition shall come, declares that ten horns
shall spring from the beast, and that another
little horn shall arise in the midst of them... "I was
looking, and this horn made war against the saints,
and prevailed against them, until the Ancient of
days came and gave judgment to the saints of the
most high God, and the time came, and the saints
obtained the kingdom."[11]

The Church Fathers and Doctors Ss. Cyril of Jerusalem (315-386
A.D.) and Augustine of Hippo (354-430 A.D.) reecho the teachings of
the Apostles. St. Cyril affirms:

After these shall rise antichrist... and having
by the signs and lying wonders of his magical
deceit, beguiled the Jews, as though he were the
expected Christ, he shall afterwards characterize
himself by all kinds of excesses of cruelty and
lawlessness... And he shall perpetrate such things
for three years and six months.[12]

---

[11]   St. Irenaeus of Lyons, *Adversus Haereses*, Book v, Ch.25, 1-3.

[12]   *The Catechetical Lectures of S. Cyril, Archbishop of Jerusalem*, A Library of the Fathers,
Oxford, 1845, Cat. 15, p.190.

St. Augustine refers to Antichrist the man of whom St. Paul speaks:

> Appoint O Lord, a lawgiver over them. This if I
> am not mistaken, will be the Antichrist to whom
> the Apostle (Paul) refers in the words: "When
> the man of sin shall be revealed." Let the Gentiles
> know themselves to be but men; and since they
> refuse to be set free by the Son of God... let
> them be slaves to a human being... since they
> themselves are but men.[13]

3.2   Early Ecclesiastical Writers

We discover in the 2nd and 3rd centuries that the early
Ecclesiastical Writers St. Hippolytus (170-235) and Lactantius (250-
317 A.D.) describe Antichrist as *a man. Hippolytus writes:*

> The Savior came into the world in the
> circumcision, and he too will come in the same
> manner... The Savior appeared in the form of
> man, and he too will come in the form of man.
> The Savior appeared in the form of a temple, and
> he too will raise a temple of stone in Jerusalem...
> Antichrist who is to raise the kingdom of the
> Jews... And in speaking of the "horns being like
> a lamb," he [St. John] means that *he will make
> himself like the Son of God, and set himself forward
> as king. And the terms "he spoke like a dragon"
> mean... "he exercised all the power of the first beast
> before him, and caused the earth and them which
> dwell therein to worship the first beast, whose deadly
> wound was healed... He will give life unto the
> image, and the image of the beast will speak... And*

---

[13]   *The Ancient Christian Writers*, St. Augustine On the Psalms, Dame Scholastica
Hebgin & Dame Felicita Corrigan, Vol. 1, Psalms 1-29. The Newman Press,
Westminster, Maryland 1960, p.125.

he will cause all… to receive a mark in their right
hand or in their forehead."[14]

Therefore thus saith the Lord God: Because thou
hast set thine heart as the heart of God: behold,
therefore I will bring strangers upon thee… and
they shall level thy beauty to destruction; and
they shall bring thee down; and thou shall die by
the death of the wounded in the midst of the sea.
Wilt thou yet say before them that slay thee, I
am God? *But thou art a man, and no God, in the*
hand of them that wound thee. Thou shalt die the
deaths of the uncircumcised by the hand of strangers;
for I have spoken it, saith the Lord.[15]

Lactantius affirms:

The Son of the most high and mighty God… shall
have destroyed unrighteousness, and executed
His great judgment, and shall have recalled to life
the righteous, who… will be engaged among men
a thousand years, and will rule them with most
just command… Also *the prince of devils, who is*
the contriver of all evils, shall be bound with chains,
and shall be imprisoned during the thousand years of
the heavenly rule in which righteousness shall reign
in the world, so that he may contrive no evil against
the people of God …[16]

---

[14] Hippolytus, in "The Ante-Nicene Fathers," Vol. V, authorized edition, WM.
B. Eerdmans Publishing Company, Grand Rapids, MI, 1978. Extant Works and
fragments, Dogmatical and Historical, Part II—*Treatise on Christ and Antichrist*, nn.
6, 25, 49.

[15] Hippolytus, Ibid., n.18.

[16] Lactantius, "The Divine Institutes", *The Ante-Nicene Fathers* (Peabody, MA:
Henrickson Pub., 1995), Vol. 7, p. 211.

Extracts of the writings of the early Church Fathers, Writers and Doctors reveal the characteristics of Antichrist: He is a man "born of fornication,"[17] "who makes use of magic, and produces lifelike apparitions… who will bring down fire from heaven, and make images speak for the demon can cause their lips to move… To all appearance he will recall the dead spirit… He will cause images and babes of a month old to speak. The followers of antichrist will question these statues or babies and they will make answer concerning this lord who has come in the latter times, affirming that he is the savior. The devil will move their lips and form the words they utter when they declare the antichrist to be the true savior of the world and this way he will cause the destruction of many souls… The temporal lords and ecclesiastical prelates for fear of losing their power or position will be on his side, since there will exist neither king nor prelate unless he wills it."[18] He will inflict punishment and death on those who refuse him worship and assuredly "raise the kingdom of the Jews,"[19] who will hail him as the long awaited Messiah.

Antichrist, "the man," through diabolic powers aided by a world government will proclaim himself god and put Christians to death. The prophet Daniel, Ss. Ephraem (306-373 A.D.), Cyril of Jerusalem, John Chrysostom (327-407 A.D.) and Jerome (347-419 A.D.) refer to this world government as the "Roman Empire" come back to life.[20] That which distinguishes the late Roman Empire from its future revival is its having for the first time "established dominion upon the entire earth, even to its

---

[17]   St. John Damascene, *De Fide Orthodoxa*, in "The Fathers of the Church," Vol. 37 (Pub: The Fathers of the church, Inc. N.Y. Trans. By Federick H. Chase, Jr. 1958) pp. 398-400.

[18]   *The Angel of Judgment*, St. Vincent Ferrer. Ave Maria Press, Notre Dame, IN (1954) pp.103 &108, edited by Mary Catherine.

[19]   Hippolytus, Ibid., nn. 6, 25.

[20]   Dn. 2:40; cf. also the Church Doctor St. Ephraem (306-373), *The Sunday Sermons of the Great Fathers*, Vol. 4, Translated and edited by M.F. Toal, Henry Regnery Co. 1964, p.355; *The Catechetical Instructions of S. Cyril, Archbishop of Jerusalem*, A Library of the Fathers, Oxford, p.190; St. Chrysostom's commentary *On II Thess.; Corpus Christianorum, Series Latina*, Vol. LXXV A, *S. Heironymi Presbyteri Opera, Pars I, Commentariorum in Danielem*, Pub: Turnholti, Typographi Brepol, Editores Pontifici, 1964 p.844.

ends."[21] Thus the revived Roman Empire signals the first historic, global victory of the powers of evil. In describing its ascension Jerome reveals:

> Ten kings shall have divided the territory of the Romans between themselves and, an eleventh man shall rise to the kingship of a small kingdom, who when he shall have overcome three of the ten kings… the other seven kings shall submit their necks to the victor.[22]

3.3   Church Doctors

The evil nations that attempt to remove God from society discover their leadership in the Antichrist whom several Church Doctors identify as a diabolic male individual. The Church Doctor St. Robert Bellarmine (1542-1621 A.D.) entitled the second heading of his work *De Summo Pontefice*, Antichrist is sure to be a certain individual man of the future! It was for the purpose of refuting the skewed conception of the papacy in his day that St. Bellarmine penned his treatise:

> For all Catholics actually perceive Antichrist to be one certain man, but all the previously referenced heretics in a manner peculiar to them teach Antichrist not to be a single person, but rather the antichrist to be a single throne, or tyrannical kingdom, or the apostolic chair of those who preside over the [Catholic] Church.[23]

[21] *The Sunday Sermons of the Great Fathers*, Fr. M.F. Toal, Regnery Pub, Chicago 1958.

[22] *Corpus Christianorum, Series Latina*, Vol. LXXV A, *S. Heironymi Presbyteri Opera, Pars I, Commentariorum in Danielem*, Pub: Turnholti, Typographi Brepol, Editores Pontifici, 1964 p.844.

[23] Bellarmini, *Opera Omnia, Disputationem Roberti Bellarmini. De Controversiis, Christianae Fidei*, Tomus Primus, Liber Tertius, De Summo Pontefice. Caput II, Antichristum certum quemdam hominem futurum, Liber Tertius 1577, p.145.

Bellarmine's teaching was inspired by the angelic Doctor St. Thomas Aquinas who wrote his *Summa Theologica three centuries earlier. In his Summa Thomas describes Antichrist as follows:*

> As in Christ dwelt the fullness of the godhead, so in Antichrist is the fullness of all wickedness. Not indeed as if his humanity were assumed by the devil into the unity of person, as the humanity of Christ is by the Son of God; but that the devil by suggestion infuses his wickedness *more copiously into him than into all others.*[24]

In later centuries, Antichrist's identity would resurface in the writings of the eighteenth century Church Doctor St. Alphonsus Maria de Liguori (1696-1787 A.D.). Alphonsus reaffirms the individual character of Antichrist:

> The devil always managed to get rid of the Mass by means of the heretics, making them the precursors of the Antichrist who, above all else, will manage to abolish, and in fact will succeed in abolishing as a punishment for the sins of men, the Holy Sacrifice of the Altar, precisely as Daniel predicted.[25]

3.4   Magisterium

The Archbishop of Bologna, Italy, Cardinal Giacomo Biffi carried St. Alphonsus' teaching into the twentieth century. On March 10, 2000 Cardinal Biffi who is a member of the Congregations for the Doctrine of the Faith, commented on the writings of Vladimir Sergeevic Solovëv (1853-1900 A.D.), a famous Russian theologian, philosopher

---

[24]   *Summa Theologica*, Thomas Aquinas, Part III, Q. 8, Art. 8, Benzinger Bros. New York 1947, Vol. II, p.2081.

[25]   *Call of Ages*, Dr. Thomas Petrisko, Queenship Publishing Co., 1995, p.331.

and prophet. Cardinal Biffi stated as credible Solovёv's prediction of the appearance of Antichrist after the 20th century, which would be marked by horrific wars and the demise of sovereign nations. According to the Cardinal, Antichrist would espouse a world religion and false ecumenism, replacing traditional religion with New Age spirituality. The Cardinal was reported in the London Times as having stated, "the Antichrist will fool many people because he will be viewed as a humanitarian with a fascinating personality, who espouses vegetarianism, pacifism, human rights and environmentalism."[26]

Pope John Paul II praised the insights and prophetic vision of Solovёv on July 30, 2000 at Castelgandolfo and in the Roman Catholic Journal *Osservatore Romano*.[27] Solovёv was a friend of Dostoevsky whom the Swiss theologian Hans Urs von Balthasar regarded as "perhaps second only to Thomas Aquinas as the greatest artist of order and organization in the history of thought."[28] His work entitled *Three Conversations: War, Progress, and the End of History, Including a Short Story of the Antichrist*, relates the unveiling of the Antichrist who disguises himself under a mask of Christianity. According to Solovёv, Antichrist is not just a personification of evil but "a religious imposter." He will arise when the twenty-first century unified states of Europe reasserts itself and fosters the replacement of traditional religion with a vague "spiritualism." Antichrist will arise "among the few believing spiritualists." He will be a man described as believing in "good, God and the Messiah," but always for the advancement of his "immense self-love." He considers himself the final Savior and benefactor of the humanity Christ came to reform but could not. Thus he sees himself as the great humanitarian who mends the great divisions wrought by Christ and his Christian followers. In his commentary on Solovёv, Bernard McGinn remarks:

---

[26] London Times, Friday, March 10, 2000; cf. also BBC News, article of March 6, 2000 Cardinal: *Antichrist is Vegetarian* by David Willey, http://news.bbc.co.uk/1/hi/world/europe/668048.stm.

[27] *Osservatore Romano*, Vatican City, Europe, August, 2000.

[28] Hans Urs von Bathlasar, *The Glory of the Lord: A Theological Aesthetics. III: Studies in Theological Styles: Lay styles* (San Francisco: Ignatius, 1986), p. 284.

As he waits for a divine sign that will enable him to effect his work of saving humanity, Antichrist confronts what for him is the ultimate temptation—to turn to Christ, risen from the dead, to ask him what to do at this crucial moment. Refusing to believe in the resurrection and unwilling to bow before Christ, the Antichrist throws himself from a precipice in a suicide attempt, only to be borne up by the devil, who adopts him as his son and surrenders to him all his power.[29]

Pope Pius XI (1857-1939 A.D.) alerts the faithful to the subversive secret organizations that assist Antichrist is his ascension to global power, which early Tradition refers to as the Beast:

There is another explanation for the rapid diffusion of the communistic ideas now (1937) seeping into every nation, great and small, advanced and backward, so that no corner of the earth is free from them. This explanation is to be found in a propaganda so truly diabolical that the world has perhaps never witnessed its like before. *It is directed from one common center.* It is shrewdly adapted to the varying conditions of diverse peoples. It has at its disposal great financial resources, gigantic organizations, international congresses, and countless trained workers. It makes use of pamphlets and reviews, of cinema, theatre and radio, of schools and even universities. Little by little it penetrates into all classes of the people and even reaches the better-minded groups of the community, with

[29] Alexander Bakshy, *War, Progress and the End of History, Including a Short Story of the Antichrist: Three Conversations by Vladimir Soloviev* (London: University of London Press, 1915) p.190-193, in Bernard McGinn, *AntiChrist, Two Thousand Years of the Human Fascination with Evil* (San Francisco: Harper, 1994), p. 266.

the result that few are aware of the poison which increasingly pervades their minds and hearts.

A third powerful factor... is the conspiracy of silence on the part of a large section of the non-Catholic press of the world. We say conspiracy, because it is impossible otherwise to explain how a press usually so eager to exploit even the little daily incidents of life has been able to remain silent for so long... and that it should have relatively so little to say concerning a world organization... This silence is due in part to short-sighted policy, and is favored by various occult forces which for a long time have been working for the overthrow of the Christian Social Order.

When the Apostles asked the Savior why they had been unable to drive the evil spirit from a demoniac, Our Lord answered: "This kind is not cast out but by Prayer and Fasting." So, too, the evil which today torments humanity can be conquered only by a world-wide holy crusade of prayer and penance. We ask especially the contemplative Orders, men and women, to redouble their prayers and sacrifices to obtain from Heaven efficacious aid for the Church in the present struggle. Let them implore also the powerful intercession of the Immaculate Virgin who, having crushed the head of the serpent of old, remains the sure Protectress and Invincible "Help of Christians."[30]

---

[30] Pope Pius XI, Encyclical Letter on Atheistic Communism March 19, 1937, nn. 17, 18, 59. http://www.papalencyclicals.net/Pius11/ P11DIVIN.HTM

CHAPTER 4

THE ANTICHRIST
BEFORE THE ERA OF PEACE

Solovёv's predictions of a 21st century Antichrist were inspired by the works of the early eastern Church Fathers and Writers. In describing Antichrist as the "False Prophet" of Revelation 19 who appears in the seven thousandth year of man's existence, Ss. Clement of Rome, Irenaeus and Hippolytus, much like Solovёv, allude to his eschatological appearance before the 1,000 years of peace in Revelation 20. These and other early Church Fathers, Writers and Doctors persuasively portray a future Era of Peace and an exalted type of Christian holiness, when the False Prophet and the Beast are cast into the fiery lake and God's will triumphantly reigns in man. It is during this Era of Peace and holiness that man, beasts and all creation will abide in harmony.[31]

I limit myself to a few extracts from Sacred Scripture, the early Ecclesiastical Writers and Saints that illustrate Antichrist's eschatological appearance before an era of universal peace. The 19th chapter of the Book of Revelation reveals:

> The beast was caught and with it the false
> prophet who had performed in its sight the signs
> by which he led astray those who had accepted

---

[31] For more information on the Era of Peace, I refer you to Chapter 5: *Era of Peace and the Reign of the Divine Will.* For a listing of the characteristics of the Era of Peace I refer you to the ecclesiastically approved book, *The Splendor of Creation,* Rev. J. Iannuzzi, St. Andrew's Productions, McKees Rocks, PA 15136, tel. (412) 787-9735.

the mark of the beast and those who had worshipped its image. The two were thrown alive into the fiery pool burning with sulfur… Then I saw an angel come down from heaven, holding in his hand the key to the great abyss and a heavy chain. He seized the dragon, the ancient serpent, which is the Devil or Satan, and tied him up for a thousand years and threw it into the abyss, which he locked and sealed, so that it could no longer lead the nations astray until the thousand years are completed… I also saw the souls of those who… had not worshipped the beast or its image nor had the accepted its mark… They came to life and they reigned with Christ for a thousand years… When the thousand years are completed, Satan will be released from his prison. He will go out to deceive the nations at the four corners of the earth, Gog and Magog, to gather them for battle.[32]

We find in the writings of St. Irenaeus of Lyons numerous references to Antichrist often scattered and uncoordinated. Allusions to manifestations of the spirit of Satan both before the Era of Peace and after the era are often found in his writings with little or no nominal distinction. It is on account of his ambiguities that academics have associated Irenaeus' teachings with millenarianism. For purposes of brevity I recall Irenaeus' allusions to Antichrist the False Prophet before the Era of Peace:

> When he (Antichrist) is come, and of his own accord concentrates in his own person the apostasy, and accomplishes whatever he shall do according to his own will and choice, sitting also in the temple of God, so that his dupes may adore him as the Christ; wherefore also shall he deservedly "be cast into the lake of fire"… After this he (St. John) likewise describes his armour-bearer, whom he *also terms a false prophet:* "He

---

[32]   Rev 19:20-20:4-5.7-8.

spake as a dragon, and exercised all the power of the first beast in his sight..."[33]

But when this Antichrist shall have devastated all things in this world, he will reign for three years and six months, and sit in the temple at Jerusalem; and then the Lord will come... *sending this man and those who follow him into the lake of fire; but bringing in for the righteous the times of the kingdom, that is, the rest, the hallowed seventh day (the era of peace).*[34]

St. Hippolytus reveals Antichrist the False Prophet whom St. John's places before the Era of Peace:

John thus speaks: "And I beheld another beast coming out of the earth; and he had two horns, like a lamb, and he spake as a dragon. And he exercised all the power of the first beast before him... *By the beast, then, coming up out of the earth, he means the kingdom of Antichrist; and by the two horns he means him and the false prophet after him. And in speaking of "the horns being like a lamb," he means that he will make himself like the Son of God, and set himself forward as king. And the terms, "he spake like a dragon," mean that he is a deceiver, and not truthful. And the words, "he exercised all the power of the first beast before him, and caused the earth and them which dwell therein to worship the first beast, whose deadly wound was healed," signify that, after the manner of the law of Augustus, by whom the empire of Rome was established, he too*

---

[33]   St. Irenaeus, Fragments, Book V, Ch. 28, 2, in The Early Church Fathers and Other Works, originally published by Wm. B. Eerdmans Pub. Co. in English in Edinburgh, Scotland, beginning in 1867. (LNPF II/XI, Schaff and Wace).

[34]   St. Irenaeus, Ibid., Book V, Ch. 30, 4.

> *will rule and govern, sanctioning everything by it,*
> *and taking greater glory to himself.*[35]

The 4th century Ecclesiastical Writer Commodianus describes Antichrist the False Prophet who arises before the Era of Peace:

> He does many wonders, since he is *the false*
> *prophet.* Especially that they may believe him,
> his image shall speak. The Almighty has given it
> power to appear such. The Jews, recapitulating
> Scriptures from him, exclaim at the same time to
> the Highest that they have been deceived.[36]

The early Ecclesiastical Writer Lactantius (250-317 A.D.) also foretells the rise of an Antichrist figure before the glorious Era of Peace:

> The prince of devils, who is the contriver of
> all evils, shall be bound with chains, and *shall*
> *be imprisoned during the thousand years* of the
> heavenly rule in which righteousness shall reign
> in the world, so that he may contrive no evil
> against the people of God (emphasis added).[37]

St. Hildegard of Bingen (1098-1179) began to receive visions at the age of forty-two and write them down, and then explain them in a work entitled *Scivias ("know the ways of the Lord").* Her visions of an individual Antichrist are one of the most inventive of the entire medieval period. Scivias can be described as a treatise on cosmic theology, as it presents God's creation of the world and the course of human history in the optic of God's divine design. It is within this framework that Hildegard presents Antichrist. She describes the birth of Antichrist from the Church. From

---

[35] Hippolytus, The Ante-Nicene Fathers, Ibid., *Treatise on Christ and Antichrist,* 48, 49.

[36] Commodianus, Ibid., Commodianus Instructions in Favor of Christian Discipline Against the Gods of the Heathens, *Of the Time of Antichrist,* XLI.

[37] Lactantius, *The Divine Institutes,* Ibid.

a vast female figure that represents the Church there emerges the horrible monstrous head of the Antichrist. According to Hildegard Antichrist will be born from the Church, he will persecute believing Christians, and he will pretend that he is divine by literally ascending into heaven. Antichrist will create a parody of the great events of the end of Christ's life, that is, his death, Resurrection, Ascension into heaven, and sending of the Holy Spirit. For Hildegard, Antichrist will pretend to die and then, in a culminating moment, when he tries to ascend into heaven, he'll be cast down and destroyed.

St. Vincent Ferrer (1350-1419 A.D.) reveals the False Prophet as the precursor to the last and fiercest Antichrist who arises after the Era of Peace:

> When *the false prophet, the precursor of Antichrist*
> comes, all who are not confirmed will apostatize,
> while those who are confirmed will stand fast in
> their faith.[38]

The first unveiling of Satan is all the more striking in view of St. Vincent Ferrer's chronology. St. Vincent Ferrer, O.P., who had several ecclesiastically recognized visions, confirms the traditional prophecies that place Antichrist before and after the Era of Peace. Vincent speaks of two Antichrists, "mixtus" and "purus," between whose appearances the Church would be renewed under a true pope and return to the evangelical counsel of poverty that Christ embraced.[39] After the first Antichrist there is the perfect age of the Church, in which all mankind returns to belief in

---

[38]   St. Vincent Ferrer, Ibid. St. Vincent states that there will be two antichrists: purus and mixtus, the former appearing before the period of universal peace and the latter following. His statement seems to second St. Hippolytus' definition of the false prophet of Rev 20, who arises "before" the era of peace. This may explain his placement of the false prophet (*purus*) "before" Satan's final appearance after the era of peace (*mixtus*), both of whom he refers to as "antichrists."

[39]   St. Vincent Ferrer, *Mirabile Opsuculum de Fine Mundi*, 1483, no place of publication reported (in Marjorie Reeves, *Prophecy in the Later Middle Ages. A Study of Joachimism*, Oxford, Clarendon, 1969, p.171, n.2).

Christ. Enter Satan's final battle against God through the second and final eschatological Antichrist.[40]

Several of the Church's saints and blesseds embellish Vincent's teachings by placing an antichristian tribulation *before* the awe-inspiring Era of Peace. *Blessed Pope Pius IX (1792-1878 A.D.) reveals:*

> There will be a great prodigy which will fill the world with awe. But this prodigy will be preceded by the triumph of a revolution during which the Church will go through ordeals that are beyond description.[41]

St. John Vianney (1786-1859 A.D.):

> A civil war shall break out everywhere. These wicked people... will imprison very many [persons], and will be guilty of more massacres. They will attempt to kill all priests and all the religious. But this shall not last long. People will imagine that all is lost; but the good God shall save all. It will be like a "sign" of the last judgment... Religion shall flourish again better than ever before.[42]

Blessed Elizabeth Canori-Mora (1774-1825 A.D.) affirms:

> Countless legions of demons shall overrun the earth... After the frightful punishment I saw a great light appear upon the earth which was

---

[40] St. Vincent Ferrer, "Sermo de Sancto Domenico", *Sermones de Sanctis*, Reeves, Antwerp, 1573, p. 299 (in O'Connor, Fr. Edward D., *Marian Apparitions Today, why So Many?*, Queenship Pub. Co. CA., 1996).

[41] Blessed Pope Pius IX, 19th Century, in Yves Dupont, *Catholic Prophecy, The Coming Chastisement*, Tan Books and Pub., Inc., IL, 1973, p.13.

[42] St. John Vianney, *The Christian Trumpet*, Fr. Pellegrino, Thos B. Noonan & Co., Boston, 1873, pp.87-88.

the sign of reconciliation of God with men.
All men shall become Catholics, and they shall
acknowledge the Pope as the Vicar of Jesus
Christ.[43]

Not only does Scripture indicate an antichristian rebellion and chastisement of nonbelievers before the universal Era of Peace, in which the good will suffer with the bad, it implies a sharing in the crown of martyrdom: "Each of the martyrs was given a long white robe, and they were told to be patient a little while longer until the quota was filled of their fellow servants and brothers to be slain, as they had been."[44] More consoling are the words taken from the Church's Catechism on the fruits of the martyr's baptism of blood that opens to them the doors of heaven:

> The Baptism of blood, like the desire for Baptism,
> brings about the fruits of Baptism without being
> a sacrament...[45]

The writings of Venerable Conchita de Armida (1862-1937 A.D.) reaffirm the martyr's immediate admission into heaven. Jesus reveals to Conchita:

> Are not the martyrs perhaps saved by the
> Baptism of blood in the bodies? Do they not
> confess the faith with the constancy of their
> pains? *Is not heaven immediately opened to them,*
> because their torments, united to Mine, purify
> them by the divine influence of the fruitfulness of
> the Father? (emphasis added)[46]

---

[43]   Blessed Elizabeth Canori-Mora, in *Catholic Prophecy*, Ibid.

[44]   Rev 6:11.

[45]   *Catechism of the Catholic Church*, Libreria Editrice Vaticana, St. Paul Books & Media, 1994, art. 1258.

[46]   Venerable Concepciòn Cabrera de Armida, *To My Priests [A Mis Sacerdotes]*, (Cleveland, OH: Archangel Crusade of Love, 1996) p.262.

From this viewpoint, the appearance of Antichrist before the Era of Peace becomes a matter of Tradition. As we have seen, the early Church presents two incarnations of "the spirit of Antichrist" as a biblical representation respectively traceable to the 19th and 20th chapters of the Book of Revelation. Because it is in Scripture and in the writings of the early Church, it is part and parcel of the Church's early Tradition.

4.1   The First Tribulation & Triumph

Below I present a collection of the ecclesiastically approved writings that illustrate the characteristics of the tribulation before the Era of Peace. It is noteworthy that these characteristics do not necessarily reflect the order in which they occur, nor are they events exclusive to the period prior to the Era of Peace, and this by virtue of the principle of biblical parallels. In his book entitled Il Libro Della Speranza (Padova, 1989), the biblical scholar Fr. Martino Penasa affirms that the hermeneutical key to interpreting the many symbolisms in Scripture is biblical parallels. These parallels, found in both the Old and New Testaments, have gained the approval of scores of professors and theologians from the universities of Rome whose ecclesiastical endorsements are prefaced in his book. Biblical parallels suggest that with each manifestation of the 'spirit of Antichrist' there follows an intensification evil, and often a series of diabolical events patterned after the preceding manifestation.

Several saints beheld in mystical vision a great tribulation within the Church, marked by antichristian uprising and a chastisement. They also witnessed an historic era of worldwide Christianity and holiness only after the tribulation. St. Bridget of Sweden (1303-1373 A.D.)[47] expected a terrible chastisement upon a world that would turn its back on God, to be followed by a great epoch of great holiness.[48] St. Hildegard[49] beheld

---

[47]   *St. Bridget of Sweden,* Johannes Jorgenson (London: Longmans, Green, 1954), vol. I, inter alia.

[48]   *Prophecy in the Latter Middle Ages,* Ibid., p. 338.

[49]   Born at Böckelheim on the Nahe, St. Hildegard (1098-1179) became a great seeress and prophetess, commonly known as the Sibyl of the Rhine. A weak and sickly child,

a chastisement that would befall a world led by the spirit of Antichrist in the form of wars, plagues and a comet. She predicted that after this chastisement the earth would experience a period of peace and holiness.

4.1.1   Schism

Sacred Scripture and approved prophetic revelations predict within the Church an imminent crisis. It will be precipitated by a split within the hierarchy of the Catholic Church and accompany the Roman Pontiff's flight from Rome. God reveals through his prophet Zechariah:

> "Awake, O sword, against my shepherd, against the man who is close to me!" declares the Lord Almighty. Strike the shepherd, and the sheep will be scattered, and I will turn my hand against the little ones. I will strike the shepherd and the sheep shall be scattered.[50]

Ezekiel prophesies the church temporarily bereft of the guidance of its shepherd on account of the poor leadership of Church hierarchy:

> You have not strengthened the weak or healed the sick or bound up the injured. You have not brought back the strays or searched for the lost. You have ruled them harshly and brutally. So they were scattered because there was no shepherd... My sheep wandered... they were scattered over the whole earth, and no one searched or looked for them. Therefore, you shepherds, hear the word of the Lord: As surely as I live, declares the Sovereign Lord, because my flock lacks a shepherd and so has

---

Hildegard was unable to read or write. Although her reading extended itself to the mere chanting of the Divine Office and singing of the Psalms, she never learned how to write. From her earliest years, God favored her with supernatural visions, including several prophetic revelations concerning the world's future.

[50]   Zec 13.9; cf. also Zec 7:14; Ps 44:11; Jer 10:21, 23:2; Lam 4:13-16; Ez 6:8.

been plundered... I am against the shepherds
and will hold them accountable for my flock. I
will remove them from tending the flock so that
the shepherds can no longer feed themselves...
I myself will search for my sheep and look after
them. As a shepherd looks after his scattered
flock when he is with them, so will I look after
my sheep. I will rescue them from all the places
where they were scattered on a day of clouds and
darkness.[51]

Other prophecies place a Church schism after the exile of a
Roman pontiff. Blessed Anne Catherine Emmerich (1774-1824 A.D.)
offers three riveting illustrations:

I had another vision of the great tribulation...
It seems to me that a concession was demanded
from the clergy that could not be granted. I
saw many older priests, especially one, who
wept bitterly. A few younger ones were also
weeping... It was as if people were splitting into
two camps.[52]

I was taken to Rome where the Holy Father,
plunged in affliction, is still concealed in order
to elude dangerous exigencies. His chief reason
for lying concealed is because he can trust so
few... The Pope is so feeble that he can no
longer walk alone... The *little black man in Rome*,
whom I often see so often, has many working
for him without their clearly knowing for what
end. He has his agents in the new black church
also. If the Pope leaves Rome, the enemies of the
Church will get the upper hand... I saw them
intercepting or turning away the roads that led

---

[51] Ez 34:4-12.

[52] *The Life and Revelations of Anne Catherine Emmerich*, Very Rev. Carl E. Schmöger
(Rockford: Tan) message dated April 12, 1820.

to the Pope. When they did succeed in getting a Bishop according to their liking, I saw that he had been intruded contrary to the will of the Holy Father; consequently, he possessed no legitimate authority... I saw the Holy Father very prayerful and Godfearing, his figure perfect, though worn out by old age and manifold sufferings, his head sunk on his breast as if in sleep. He often fainted away and seemed to be dying, I often saw him supported by apparitions during his prayer, and then his head was upright.[53]

I saw enlightened Protestants, plans formed for the blending of religious creeds, the suppression of papal authority... I saw no Pope, but a bishop prostrate before the High Altar. In this vision I saw the church bombarded by other vessels... It was threatened on all sides... They built a large, extravagant church which was to embrace all creeds with equal rights... but in place of an altar were only abomination and desolation. Such was the new church to be...[54]

Blessed Anna-Maria Taigi (1769-1837 A.D.) was exceptionally endowed with many supernatural revelations that are ecclesiastically approved. She accurately predicted the deaths of famous personages and many historical events. On one occasion, she said of Pope Leo XIII who lay on his deathbed, "the Pope will not die, but Monsignor Strambi should prepare himself since he has offered his life for the Pope and Our Lord has accepted his generous offering." Miraculously, within a few days Pope Leo XIII, who was in the worst of health, made a total recovery, while Monsignor Strambi, who was enjoying the best of health, died. Blessed Anne-Maria prophesied the exile of the Roman Pontiff:

[53] Ibid., Vol. II, pp. 290, 292, 303, 310.

[54] Ibid., Vol. II, pp. 346, 349, 353.

> Religion shall be persecuted, and priests massacred. Churches shall be closed, but only for a short time. The Holy Father shall be obliged to leave Rome.[55]

St. Pope Pius X (1835-1914 A.D.) reaffirms Blessed Anna-Maria's vision:

> I saw one of my successors taking to flight over the bodies of his brethren. He will take refuge in disguise somewhere; and after a short retirement [exile] he will die a cruel death.[56] The present wickedness of the world is only the beginning of the sorrows which must take place before the end of the world.[57]

Venerable Bartholomew Holzhauser (1613-1658 A.D.) reveals that during the persecution Rome will be devastated:

> God will permit a great evil against the Church: Heretics and tyrants will come suddenly and unexpectedly; they will break into the Church while bishops, prelates and priests are asleep. They will enter Italy and lay Rome waste;

---

[55] Blessed Anna-Maria Taigi, in *Catholic Prophecy*, p.45. Although the Pope may have to flee Rome and remain in exile and, as St. Pope Pius X says, there die a cruel death, he will be succeeded by another validly elected Pope. Blessed Anna-Maria Taigi describes the events that culminate in a new, valid papal election. After the Church has been without a Pope for some time, a new conclave will be convened to elect his valid successor: "*After the three days of darkness, St. Peter and St. Paul, having come down from heaven [understood in a metaphoric sense] will preach in the whole world and designate a new Pope. A great light will flash from their bodies and will settle upon the cardinal who is to become Pope. Christianity, then, will spread throughout the world*" (Ibid.).

[56] If the pontiff will die "a cruel death," it is not a death without God's divine assistance. Some of the greatest spiritual giants underwent deaths deemed by many in a certain sense as cruel, beginning with Jesus Christ himself.

[57] Saint Pope Pius X, 20th century, in *Catholic Prophecy*, p.22.

they will burn down the churches and destroy
everything.[58]

In the approved messages of Our Lady of La Salette the Blessed
Virgin Mary revealed to the two children Melanie Calvat and Maximin
Giraud that Rome will become the seat of Antichrist:

> Rome will lose the faith and become the seat of Antichrist.[59]

St. Leopold Mandic (1866-1942 A.D.), a Capuchin priest from
Croatia, states that during the tribulation the Church of the USA will
create a schism by separating itself from the Church of Rome. He wrote
to an American priest in 1939:

> Be careful to preserve your faith, because in the
> future the Church in the U.S.A. will be separated
> from Rome.[60]

It is imperative to emphasize the charism of infallibility that Jesus
Christ directly communicated to the Pope (Peter) for the spiritual welfare
of the faithful. This charism of the extraordinary Magisterium freely
bestowed by Christ to the Pope is exercised *ex Cathedra* (from the Bishop
of Rome's St. John Lateran Cathedral) on revelations and issues of morals
and faith.[61] The Vicar of Christ on earth – the Roman pontiff – exercises

---

[58]   Venerable Bartholomew Holzhauser, *Apocalypsin*, 1850, in Catholic Prophecy, Ibid.,
       p.40.

[59]   Message of Our Lady of LaSalette dated September 19, 1846. After a thorough
       investigation, the bishop of Grenoble ruled in favor of the La Salette apparitions.

[60]   Leopoldo Mandic, http://personal.lig.bellsouth.net/l/a/lasereye/may02.html.

[61]   The Apostles were commissioned by Christ to "go and teach all nations" (Mt. 28:19)
       and to "go into the whole world and preach the gospel to every creature" (Mk. 16:15).
       The means, therefore, established by Christ for the propagation of his teaching is not
       so much writing, but oral preaching, a living *Magisterium* (preaching and teaching
       office), to which he assures his personal assistance to the end of the world: "Go
       therefore, and make disciples of all nations... teaching them to observe all things
       that I have commanded you. And behold, I am with you always, until the end of the
       world" (Mt. 28:20). These words also show that the Magisterium founded by Christ

the extraordinary Magisterium. Christ gave this charism to the Pope so that the faithful may have the infallible assurance that what he teaches on morals and faith is indeed the unchanging Word of God, and not the word of man. The ordinary Magisterium is the episcopal sharing of this gift. Though the college of bishops may "participate" in the exercise of the pontiff's supreme gift of infallibility through a sharing in his singular authority, their authority depreciates when divorced from it. The laity, for their part, are to lend loyal respect to both the pope and the bishops in union with him.[62] Whence the Magisterium emerges as the teaching office of the Catholic Church expressed through the pope and college of bishops to enlighten its members on God's revealed truths.

Therefore, when God's prophets foretell a shepherdless Church they are not in contempt of papal or episcopal authority, but are alerting the faithful to a period in which the pope will either be exiled or killed, and during his temporary vacancy, the office of papacy may be openly spurned, or an invalid papal election may occur. Indeed the Church has experienced several invalid papal elections, including the 14th century schism in which the two Popes Gregory XI and Clement VII claimed the throne simultaneously. Needless to say, there can be only one validly reigning pontiff, not two. So one pope was an imposter vested with false authority by a few nationalist cardinals who held an invalid conclave, namely Clement VII. What made this conclave invalid was the absence of the full body of cardinals and subsequently the required 2/3's majority vote. Yet in recent years, the late Pope John Paul II modified the voting mechanism. Traditionally, a 2/3's majority is required to elect the pope. Pope John Paul II has modified the rules so that after a little over a week's time the cardinals can elect a new pontiff by simple majority after they have gone through the whole conclave process. At present, there are 119 electoral cardinals, so in essence 60 votes can suffice for the valid election of a new pontiff, provided the full body of cardinals agrees to put this new

---

is entrusted to the apostolic college. This teaching authority which resides primarily in Peter, is shared by the Apostles and their successors, the bishops, in communion with him.

[62] *Lumen Gentium*, 25; Ccc, 2034, 2039.

modification into practice. It is worthy of mention that Pope John Paul II had appointed all but three of the recent conclave electors, to suggest that a determined majority can elect someone who is not a consensus figure. Although the late pontiff had never explained why he made the electoral voting modifications, the answer appears twofold: In a worst-case scenario, the church wouldn't be without a pope for more than a month, as the conclave opens about 16 days after the pope's death. Another, more compelling response, is that this new voting mechanism would allow more doctrinaire hard-liners to advance someone who would have run aground if they had had to achieve a 2/3's majority.

Other criteria that determine the validity of a papal election are that no conclave may be held in attempt to elect a pope so long as the true pope is alive, even if in exile, and without his expressed consent. Therefore the prophecies predicting the pope's flight or exile from Rome do not signify the pope's resignation from office, nor does it validate an attempted papal election in his absence. God never leaves his flock untended, but on account of sin he tests his flock for a short period as gold is tested in the fire in order that it may emerge purer, holier and with a stronger faith.

4.1.2   War

There are several Church-approved revelations that prophesy an imminent third world war if people do not convert. The great war is contingent; it depends upon us God-fearing Christians to change our ways and so mitigate or possibly eliminate the great war. Numerous Marian apparitions that the Church has officially recognized contain appeals from the Blessed Virgin Mary for an immediate return to God's commandments and to prayer and fasting to avoid grave danger. In the revelations to the three shepherd children of Fatima, Mary implored prayer and fasting to avoid a second world war, but as too few paid heed to her requests, the war soon followed. In the 1970's to Sister Agnes Sasagawa at Akita, Japan, Mary makes the following appeal:

> As I have already announced earlier, the Heavenly Father will send a terrible punishment over the whole world of mankind if people do

not repent and change their lives: a punishment
that will be more terrible than the great flood;
a punishment the world has never experienced.
Fire will fall from the sky and destroy the larger
part of humanity and will not spare priests and
lay people. The survivors will suffer so much that
they will envy the dead.[63]

In the Church-approved 1980 revelations of Cuapa, Nicaragua,
Mary tells Bernardo Martinez that unless we change we will experience a
third world war:

> Make peace. Do not ask our Lord for peace if
> you do not make it... Pray, pray the rosary for all
> the world. Tell believers and non believers that
> the world is threatened by grave dangers. I ask
> the Lord to appease His justice, but if you don't
> change, you will hasten the arrival of a Third
> World War.[64]

---

[63]   Albert J. Hebert, *Wonders and Response*, P.O. Box 309, Paulina, LA,1988, p. 128.
The extraordinary events began on June 12, 1973, when Sister Agnes Sasagawa saw
brilliant mysterious rays emanate suddenly from the tabernacle. The same thing
happened on each of the two days that followed. On June 28, 1973, a cross-shaped
wound appeared on the inside left hand of Sr. Agnes. It bled profusely and caused
her much pain. On July 6, Sister Agnes heard a voice coming from the statue of the
Blessed Virgin Mary in the chapel where she was praying. The statue was carved
from a single block of wood from a Katsura tree and is three feet tall. On the same
day, a few of the sisters noticed drops of blood flowing from the statue's right hand.
On four occasions, this act of blood flow repeated itself. The wound in the statue's
hand remained until September 29, when it disappeared. On September 29, the day
the wound on the statue disappeared, the sisters noticed the statue had now begun
to "sweat", especially on the forehead and neck. On August 3, Sister Agnes received
a second message. On October 13, she received a final third message. Two years later
on January 4, 1975, the statue of the Blessed Virgin began to weep. It continued to
weep at intervals for the next 6 years and eight months. It wept on 101 occasions.

[64]   Cuapa, Nicaragua, message of Mary to Bernardo Martinez, May 1980, Blue Army,
Washington, NJ. In 1982 the apparitions of Mary at Cuapa, Nicaragua received
Ecclesiastical Approvals from Mons. Bosco M. Vivas Robelo, Auxiliary Bishop and
Vicar General of Managua.

Mary reveals to Julia Kim of Naju, Korea, that the third world war is imminent:

> If you do not accept my words, and reject the
> Lord, the world will become seas of fire and
> perish through the Third World War. The God
> of love can also be the God of wrath. Pray harder
> and offer sufferings.[65]

It must be borne in mind that prophecies foretell the coming war as a progressive event: It will begin with civil disturbances and revolutions throughout Western Europe, in particular throughout Italy (Rome), France (Paris; Marseilles) and Spain. The terrorists will take advantage of the anarchy to invade these cities and countries. One will then witness the invasion of Rome, France and Spain by a "barbaric nation" that many prophecies associate with terrorist Muslim nations. These invasions will engage other nations in war.

4.1.3   Warning

Before the great chastisement, God, in his infinite mercy, provides us with every opportunity to make amends. In Jesus' many appeals, especially those of his Blessed Mother, one discovers practical steps that lead to peace with God, with one's neighbor and with the world around him. One of the graces that God will grant humankind is the revelation of its state of soul before the chastisement, so that it may have time to sufficiently prepare itself for the impending judgment. This moment in which we see ourselves as God sees us is popularly known as the "Warning." It will be a supernatural occurrence associated with an event in the sky that will cause every man, woman, and child to see the state of

---

[65]   Naju, Korea, Message of Nov. 26, 1989. http://www.marystouch.com/truth/
status.htm. In July 1989 Archbishop Yoon affirmed that the authenticity of the
tears secreted from the statue of the Blessed Virgin Mary 700 times (June 30, 1985
- January 14, 1992) was incontestable. The Archbishop has allowed the supernatural
messages Julia has received to be distributed and pilgrims to pray before the statue of
Our Lady that wept 700 times.

his or her own soul—that is, all the unrepented evil they have done and
good they have failed to do – through an illumination of conscience. It is
one of God's final appeals before the great chastisement to bring about in
us a change for the better. The Warning will be especially severe on those
that are in mortal sin, but less severe on those who are with unrepented
venial sin. Among the prophets who beheld the Warning in mystical
vision, worthy of mention is 16th century Saint Edmund Campion:

> I pronounce a great day… wherein the terrible
> Judge should reveal all men's consciences and try
> every man of each kind of religion. This is the day
> of change, this is the day which I threatened.[66]

Anna Maria Taigi, beatified in 1920, spoke of an illumination of
conscience that would be followed by a great chastisement. She indicated
that this illumination of conscience would result in the saving of many
souls because many would repent as a result of this "warning"… this
miracle of "self illumination." Saint Faustina Kowalska also experienced
this "warning" in her lifetime and describes it:

> Suddenly, I saw the complete condition of my
> soul as God sees it. I could clearly see all that is
> displeasing to God. I did not know that even the
> smallest transgressions will have to be accounted
> for.[67]

In the Church-approved revelations of Betania, Venezuela the
Blessed Virgin Mary intimates the Warning:

> There is coming the great moment of a great
> day of light. The consciences of this beloved
> people must be violently shaken so that they
> may "put their house in order" and offer to Jesus
> the just reparation for the daily infidelities that

[66] Call of Ages, Ibid., p. 181.

[67] St. Maria Faustina, *Diary of Divine Mercy*, April 30, 1928, Notebook I, 36.

are committed on the part of sinners.[68] A great
moment is approaching, a great day of light… it
is the hour of decision for mankind.[69]

4.1.4 The False Prophet and the Beast

As mentioned earlier, the False Prophet will arise before the Era
of Peace to proclaim himself God and seat himself in the throne of God,
with the assistance of the pagan united nations known as the Beast. St.
Hippolytus states that "by *the beast, then coming up out of the earth, he*
means the kingdom of Antichrist, and by the two horns he means him (the
kingdom) and the false prophet… In speaking of the 'horns being like a lamb,' he
means that he will make himself like the Son of God, and set himself forward as
king."[70] (St. Vincent Ferrer assures us that another fiercer Antichrist will
arise up after the False Prophet, after the Era of Peace, and St. Hippolytus
refers to the False Prophet as "the precursor of [the fiercest] Antichrist.)"
In the Book of Revelation Antichrist, the False Prophet, will impose what
many consider a "mark" upon the earth's citizens.

4.1.4.1 Mark of the Beast

It is noteworthy that the original Greek word for "mark" is
Káragma (χάραγμα), which does not mean "mark" at all, but more
forcefully a "strike that leaves an impression," or a "brand within the flesh."
Enter the False Prophet who imposes upon all citizens his Luciferian
brand within their right hand or forehead, whereby they may buy and
sell material goods. Those who wisely refuse the Luciferian brand will
be forced to acquire all food, clothing and shelter from the underground

---

[68]   Maria Esperanza, Volume 15-n.2 Featured Article, from www.sign.org.

[69]   *Call of Ages,* Ibid., p.190. Bishop Pio Vello Ricardo personally undertook the
investigation and declared on November 21, 1987 after informing Rome, that the
apparitions of Betania, Venezuela are authentic and supernatural in character.
Apart from the Akita, Japan (1973), these were the first apparitions approved by the
Church since Beauraing and Banneux, Belgium (1949).

[70]   Hippolytus, Ibid., 49.

Christian market. And because they are Christians they will be persecuted, hunted and, if caught, put to death by Antichrist's emissaries.

More needs to be said. Some maintain that since the Luciferian mark in the flesh may be imposed by the world government, alias the Beast, vested with authority to bind citizens by law, the lawabiding citizen may passively consent to receiving the mark without actively or materially cooperating in immorality. Analogously, they maintain, one pays federalized taxation on abortion without actively cooperating in the immoral act of abortion. Therefore should Antichrist require that all citizens receive his Luciferian mark, it would not seem immoral for the citizen to passively consent.

While this argument seems persuasive, it fails to consider the following: unlike any juridical act of government (i.e., taxation on abortion), Antichrist and his delegates will impose the penalty of death on those who so much as refuse his mark, thereby changing the so-called acts of government into acts of war and terror on all Christians. He will wage a fierce attack on all those who in refusing to accept his mark, refuse to worship him as god. His Luciferian mark will be impressed within the flesh of the right hand or forehead as a public declaration, and he will demand customary public acts of worship from all civilians. Acts of public worship will be directed toward an image that he will erect in honor of the one-world conglomerate Beast that ensured his ascension to global power. Satan will empower this image to come to life and with diabolic mechanizations, aided by computerized artificial intelligence and electronic technology, he will wield authority over the earth's inhabitants. In the days of Antichrist there will be little wiggle room for pusillanimous thinkers who expect to receive his Luciferian mark solely to obtain material goods to survive. The one who receives the mark of the beast has actively consented to idolatry and is henceforth targeted by Gods' angels for the day of wrath that will manifest itself quickly and with great violence. The Book of Revelation reveals their fate:

> The first angel went and poured out his bowl
> on the earth. Festering and ugly sores broke
> out on those who had the mark of the beast or
> worshipped his image.[71]

---

[71] Rev 16.2.

Those who have refused the mark of the beast will be put to the test, but divine assistance will give them strength. Antichrist will force them into hiding where they will pray in secret and receive the sacraments from bishops and priests in private homes or cenacles where small altars are erected, and God's angels will seal them on the forehead to protect them from his wrath. Revelation 7:4 and 14:1 reveal that a spiritual, divine seal will be imprinted on the foreheads of those that refuse the mark of the beast to guard them and equip them to endure the seven trumpets.

4.1.5   Antichrist's Resources

Antichrist will receive power from Satan, and employ modern technology in his efforts to exercise absolute control over the planet. The Russian Scientific Institute of Research Professor A.E. Akimov confirmed that in the 1980's *spin-torsion generators* were discovered. These generators were created for the purpose of influencing at the atomic and molecular levels the subtle cerebral structures in the human brain. The leading professor of the Psychotronic Russian Laboratory V. Antonov states: *"Torsion fields of technological origin can change and even shut down the crystals that influence the human psyche (such crystals are formed of intracellular matter that includes complex molecules and polymers)."*[72] Hence the so-called *psycho-torsion generator*, specifically designed to influence the consciences of individuals and masses of people, can indeed be an effective tool in the hands of Antichrist and the Beast.

The German specialist Ernest Meklenburg offers a compelling insight:

> Already in the 1960's the CIA was aware that Russia was perfecting the electromagnetic communications system aboard aeronautic ships, and teaching its astronauts how to develop the methods for telepathic transmission of information, a method that is more easily developed in space than on earth... One may

---

[72]   B.Y. Tichoplav-T.S. Tichoplav, *The Great Passage*, VES, St. Petersburg, Russia 2002, inter alia.

consider the control and manipulation of human consciences their prime objective.[73]

The CIA American psychologist Jose Delgardo underscores, "Control of the human conscience is more dangerous than the atomic bomb." In fact leading experts confirm that the gigantic power of weapon rays[74] surpasses 1000 times in power the strength of the atomic bomb. And A. Akimenko tells why: Not only can they influence human psychological patterns, at the molecular level spin-torsion generators are quite capable of turning into dust any building or military structure. "This is a very effective tool against terrorists," affirms the Russian journalist A. Kondrashov.[75]

Many leading psycho-torsion experts confirm that nearly ten satellites over different regions transmit from special antennas powerful,

---

[73] E. Meklenburg, "Psycho-Weapons and the Military Strategy of the 21st Century," in *The Terminator* Russian Newspaper (1996) nn. 1-2, pp. 6-9.

[74] "Weapons rays" is an expression that describes electromagnetic technological devices used to influence human behavior. Wade W. Smith, Deputy of Raytheon Missile Systems' Directed Energy Weapons division, Tucson, AZ, spoke of the promise of directed-energy weapons at the Photon Forum 2004 in the Loews Ventana Canyon Resort, AZ. Deputy Smith stated that like a massive laser gun mounted on a military-style Humvee, the Active Denial Technology (ADT) weapon, which uses directed energy technology, "gets the bad guy to stop what he's doing." The ADT weapon shoots a narrow beam of concentrated electromagnetic energy. Traveling at the speed of light, the energy penetrates less than 1/64 of an inch into the skin quickly heating up the skin's surface, according to the Department of Defense. The pain is nearly identical to that experienced when briefly touching a hot light bulb, but it leaves no burn mark or permanent damage. "The ADT weapon literally gets under your skin and causes high, nonlethal pain," Smith said. The technology was developed by the U.S. Air Force Research Laboratory and the Department of Defense's Joint Non-Lethal Weapons Directorate. Raytheon's Directed Energy product line has its headquarters at the missile plant on Tucson's South Side, AZ, with some of the engineering being conducted by local employees. Barbara Starr, a Raytheon spokeswoman, affirmed that most of the development on the product line, including ADT, is being conducted at the company's California plant (Tucson Citizen, April 9, 2004, article by Romano Cedillós).

[75] A. Kondrashov, article entitled *21th Century Death Rays,* in the *Arguments and Factors* Russian Newspaper, 2000, n. 24.

ultrahigh frequency (UHF) and extremely high frequency (EHF) radiation waves that are capable of influencing masses of people. Not only in Russia but also in the USA developments are progressing rapidly in the construction of a spatial psychotronic platform. "Teledesis" is a government project that includes in itself almost 300 double-destination satellites together with platform lasers in space and torsion generators within satellites that can destroy intercontinental rockets. . These satellites, through the action of radiation waves may single out any point on the planet for the specific purpose of provoking psychological changes in order to influence, if not control the way people think and act. While accumulated scientific knowledge reveals that at present, torsion generators are insufficient to wield absolute control of individual behavioral patterns, they are nonetheless effective in shutting down some of the crystals that influence the human psyche in order to produce "zombie-like" individuals for the purpose of executing government commands.[76] Recent testing demonstrates that these generators have been successful in producing behavioural reactions – sometimes unpredictable – in groups of individuals on the level of consciousness that include insecurity, fear, submission, joy, depression and anger.[77]

---

[76]   Teledesis can employ the so-called "death rays" at great distances upon any given object or individual, and has been reported to have achieved success in provoking biological alterations, illnesses in individuals, and disturbances in the earth's elements.

[77]   Official reports of psychological alteration through the abuse of weapons rays are increasing. I refer you to one example that may be found at the following site: http:// manaus.lbgo.com/. In 2002 this official report to the United Nations Secretary General, Talis Betritis provides documentation from medical experts on the bodily injuries and psychological impairments she was forced to undergo by random governmental testing. She states in this report: "Since late 1998 the Constitutional Protection Bureau (State security institution) officials are, by using technical means, effecting illegal psychotronic attacks against me... by transmitting towards me a modulated signal causing alterations in my body... a reason for loss of the organ's functions... injuries, mental harm and other sufferings... by establishing therein an image perceiving my bio-field... causing me bodily suffering, as a result of which I have lost my capacity for work. I am being caused moral, material harm... that I cannot continue my studies in the University..."

Much of the information I provide in this book may be found in publications by professors of scientific institutes especially in Russia, USA and Germany, and from experts in Psychotronic Labratories, Torsion Generators and Psychology. V.J. Tihoplav and T.S. Tihoplav have published a work entitled, "The Great Journey" in which they present much of the information that public news has not revealed.[78] For example, already 265 satellites are in place by the government and ready to connect all computers of the entire planet. These satellites are in three groups under the United States government: Lockheed-Martin (9 satellites), Hughes Electronics (28 satellites) and Teledesis (228 satellites). The estimated cost in 2005 for high velocity data communication operations via satellites is more than $20,000,000.00. The most ambitious project is that of forming a consortium of Teledesis.[79] This project foresees the kickoff of at least 228 satellites in low orbit that had already begun in 1998.

In 1995 the United States Congress ratified a budget of $10,000.000.00 for the development of Project Haarp in Alaska, which commenced operations in 1998.[80] "Haarp" stands for High Frequency Active Aural Research Project, a joint effort of the Air Force and the Navy at an isolated base near Gakona, Alaska. It uses 72-foot tall extra low frequency (ELF) antennas, 360 of which are spread out over four acres and enclosed within barbwire fencing. Put simply, the apparatus for Haarp is a reversal of a radio telescope used to penetrate the earth: Antennas send out signals instead of receiving, and Haarp is the test run whose purpose is to emit an ultrahigh frequency radio wave that lifts areas of the ionosphere, by focusing a beam that discharges heat in a given area. The electromagnetic waves may then bounce back to earth and penetrate every object of the planet, living and deceased. By this means it is able to

---

[78] V.J. Tihoplav – T.S. Tihoplav, The Great Journey, VES Publications, St. Petersburg, Russia 2002, cf. pp.126-129.

[79] The participants of this project include Microsoft, McCaw, Boeing and most recently Motorola.

[80] A. Frela, Electromagnetic Swords in Alaska, in *The Limit of Impossibility* Russian Newspaper (1999) n. 20, pp. 8-9.

locate and possibly influence all creatures great and small (Rev 13.7). The ELF antennas may already be used to create a global shield of heat (hot spots), which is required in the control of local weather. [81]

Arco Power Technologies Incorporated (APTI), a subsidiary of Atlantic Richfield Company and one of the biggest oil companies in the world, was the contractor that built the Haarp facility. Arco sold this subsidiary the patents and the second-phase construction contract to E-Systems in June 1994. E-Systems is one of the biggest intelligence contractors in the world, assisting the CIA in defense intelligence organizations and other projects. $1.8 billion of their annual sales go to these organizations, with $800 million for unclassified projects.[82] Haarp media publicity informs the working citizen that the High Frequency Active Auroral Research Program is mainly an academic project with the goal of changing the ionosphere to improve communications for our own good. It argues that it is a good idea to all who believe in sound national defense and to those concerned about cost-cutting. However, the possible uses which the Haarp reports do not explain, and which can only be found in US Air Force, Army, Navy and other federal agency records are unsettling. According to aforementioned sources, additional US military documents reveal that Haarp aims to learn how to "exploit the ionosphere for Department of Defense purposes."[83] Communicating with submarines

[81] Ibid., Weather modification is possible by, for example, altering upper atmosphere wind patterns by constructing one or more plumes of atmospheric particles, which will act as a lens or focusing device. Molecular modifications of the atmosphere can take place so that environmental effects can be achieved. Besides actually changing the molecular composition of an atmospheric region, a particular molecule or molecules can be chosen for increased presence. For example, ozone, nitrogen, etc. concentrations in the atmosphere could be artificially increased.

[82] http://www.crystalinks.com/haarp.html

[83] Ibid. The military has issued the following report on the benefits to society that the HAARP system could bring, and they are as follows: It could give the military a tool to replace the electromagnetic pulse effect of atmospheric thermonuclear devices (considered a viable military option since 1986); replace the huge Extremely Low Frequency (ELF) submarine communication system operating in Michigan and Wisconsin with a new and more compact technology; replace the over-the-horizon radar system that was once planned for the current location of HAARP with a more flexible and accurate system; provide a way to wipe out communications over

is only one of those purposes. Some scientists conclude that the potential effects from arbitrary or tyrannical use of these power levels in our natural shield, the ionosphere, could be cataclysmic. An expert in mineral geology, Professor Y. N. Ianizkiy, prophetically contests, "The planet is a living organism with a built-in intelligence to support us as we support microbes and parasites. We coexist in symbiosis. Much like us, the earth's patience is limited, such that when our harmful influence upon nature achieves its limit, the earth must take action as it has in the past."[84]

Other technological approaches being used today include Satellite Surveillance, Laser Listening Devices, Voice Translation, Interface to Nerve Cells, Micro-Chips, Bio-chips, Smart Cards and Foolproof ID. With the use of cellular towers and satellite systems, any animal or human, living or deceased, that is embedded with the now readily available micro-chip implant can be triangulated to within 10 feet of its location.

Possible threats of privacy invasion, and the usurpation of the inalienable rights come from today's world of automation and technology. I here recall a few examples. *Navstar Satellites* are in place and accurate in tracking almost anyone, anywhere on the face of the earth, without their knowledge. *Laser Listening Devices* can listen to any conversation as

an extremely large area, while keeping the military's own communications systems working; provide a wide-area earth-penetrating tomography, which, if combined with the computing abilities of EMASS and Cray computers, would make it possible to verify many parts of nuclear nonproliferation and peace agreements (This technology can confuse or completely disrupt airplanes' and missiles' sophisticated guidance systems. The ability to spray large areas of earth with electromagnetic waves of varying frequencies, and to control changes in those waves, makes it possible to knock out communications on land or sea as well as in the air. Thus, the invention provides the ability to put unprecedented amounts of power in the earth's atmosphere at strategic locations and to maintain the power injection level, particularly if random pulsing is employed, in a manner far more precise and better controlled than heretofore accomplished by the prior art, particularly by detonation of nuclear devices of various yields at various altitudes); act as a tool for geophysical probing to find oil, gas and mineral deposits over a large area; be employed to detect incoming low-level planes and cruise missiles, making other technologies obsolete.

[84] I.N. Ianizkiy, *Physics and Religion*, Moscow, Russian Physics Community Edition, The Advantage of Society Pub House, 1995, p.65.

much as 20 miles away. *Voice Translation* is a computer system that can translate a language into almost 170 other languages and dialects, and broadcast those translations by satellite around the world to efficiently aid in monitoring the earth's inhabitants. The *Smart Card* is a Fool Proof ID that holds huge amounts of data, and which would not only simplify the health care system, but also replace one's cash, credit cards, social security, passport and other personal data. The dangers of the Smart Card are the creation of a cashless society and the monitoring of everyone on the planet. That the government is quickly moving toward the Smart Card is made evident in a piece of legislation that was ratified as recent as March 2005. The bill was approved by a 261-161 House of Representatives vote. The measure, called the Real ID Act, says that driver's licenses and other ID cards must include a digital photograph, anti-counterfeiting features and undefined "machine-readable technology, with defined minimum data elements that could include a magnetic strip or RFID tag." The new legislation requires all Americans to accept a National Driver's License with ID tracking chip.

The *Bio-chip* is about the size of a grain of rice, and it is currently being implanted in animals with a needle, just under the skin. According to Jim Sellar, the President of Destron/IDI (the Boulder Colorado firm that manufactures the Implantable Biochip), the Bio-chip has replaced tags on dogs and cats, and brands and cowbells on cattle. The Bio-chip is being marketed by Infopet of Southern California and reportedly costs about $4.50 per unit. The Implantable Bio-chip is a radio transponder (which never needs batteries or replacement). And much like the Smart Card, there are dangers to the Biochip, as it can arguably be integrated with the network system of communications satellites that now orbit the earth, to possibly monitor every individual's movement, conversation and financial transactions. The *Micro-chip* is smaller than the Bio-Chip and requires a painless implant insertion just below the skin. With the implanted chip, there will be no chance of valuable financial information falling into the wrong hands. Used as a transponder, the Micro-Chip emits a signal that provides vital information as well as a location marker. *Interfaces to Nerve Cells* are electrodes made of machined silicon and laced with micro-circuitry that can interface to implants and to individual nerve cells. These micro devices can stimulate or record signals from a single nerve cell to enable a Micro-chip implant to sense and control in a whole new manner. It can be used as an internal shock collar, for the behavior modification or stimulation of animals, and possibly persons who receive them.

While these and other technological systems may provide the government and its citizens with unparalleled benefits, they can also invade the common citizen's privacy through the monitoring of its every movement, conversation and financial transaction. Indeed modern technology may become a powerful tool of Antichrist and the Beast in their quest to achieve global control of weapons, communications and commercial systems. The cutting edge of current technology may provide Antichrist and his world government with the many tools they require in their war on Christianity. Our Lord Jesus cautions us not to be deceived (Mt 24.4), and instructs us to be wise as serpents (Mt 10.16) while preparing for His return (Mk 13.32-37). Certainly, technology, or government development of electronic weapons have benefits, and in itself is not evil. However, the evil ends for which Antichrist and the Beast may use technology will render it a most powerful weapon in the hand of Satan.

4.1.6   The Two Beasts

Antichrist's ascension to global power is enunciated in the Book of Revelation 13 under the appearance of two beasts. The first beast comes out of the sea and the second beast comes up out of the earth, both vested with the power and authority of Satan. The two beasts arise shortly before the "the thousand years" Era of Peace to conquer the world. St. John describes the beasts as possessing certain traits that reveal their nature and purpose. The beast from the sea with seven heads represents the seven world leaders that ensure Antichrist's ascension to power in the city with seven hills. .[85] The beast's horns biblically represent its means of communication and amplification. Modern technology may certainly facilitate globalized communications for the Antichrist through the use

---

[85]   Rev 17:9 reveals that Antichrist will reign in the city with seven hills, and our Lady revealed at La Salette, "Rome will become the seat of Antichrist."

of satellites, tele-internet devices and other forms of mass media. By its "heads" and "horns" Antichrist will attempt through diabolic astuteness, possibly aided by technology, to subject all men, women and children to his anti-theocratic rule.

First, Antichrist will espouse a communist ideology to further Satan's plan to destroy God's Church and stifle all promptings of the Holy Spirit in the souls of God's creatures. He will assuage humanity's desire for religion by delivering to the masses as opium an idol, or god, that appeals to all religions. By the working of diabolic wonders, possibly aided by technology, he will mesmerize the masses, remove the perpetual sacrifice of the Eucharist, seat himself in the throne of the church and proclaim himself god.

Enter the second beast that comes from the earth. The second beast has "two horns like a lamb's but spoke like a dragon," and forces the earth's inhabitants to "worship the first beast."[86] In Scripture the lamb is the symbol of sacrifice in the Church and its blood removes the punishment of sin. Moreover, this symbol of sacrifice is intimately linked to the priesthood, the "two horns." The Old Testament high priest wore a headpiece with two horns, and the bishop's miter has two horns that indicate the fullness of the priesthood. When therefore Revelation presents the second beast as having two horns like a lamb, it intimates that secret society that has infiltrated the interior of the Church with its communist ideology, namely Freemasonry. Ecclesiastical Freemasonry was foretold at Fatima when Mary announced that unless people convert, communism will spread it errors throughout the world, and Satan would enter the Church even to its summit. Thus Antichrist seeks to destroy Christ and his Church to build a new idol in Christ's place, namely Antichrist and his black church.

It is noteworthy that like Communism, Freemasonry denies the existence of the Judeo-Christian God. By this denial, Freemasonry professes belief in "a" god to cleverly operate within Christian circles.

---

[86] Rev 13:11-12.

Its numerous philanthropic activities and relief-service projects serve to keep shrouded the identity of its true god, nature and purpose. For it is in tolerance and acceptance that Freemasonry thrives and penetrates within the Church's interior. Now one reason for the denial of the Judeo-Christian God is the inalienable rights and liberties that come from God as laid out in the Old and New Testaments, and articulated in the United States Constitution (i.e., right to life, freedom to express the Christian religion, freedom of assembly, etc.). These rights and liberties protect citizens from government arbitration, and do not come from the government or from the will of a party majority, but from God. Now in order for Freemasonry to control our rights and liberties, they must deny the existence of the Judeo-Christian God from whom these privileges derive. Enter the atheistic world government, or the Beast, which usurps our rights and liberties and declares them privileges bestowed on us by the government.

The Catholic Church has repeatedly condemned all ties with Freemasonry. Eight popes have issued pronouncements condemning Freemasons or those activities and principles identified with Freemasonry: Popes Clement XII, Benedict XIV, Pius VII, Leo XII, Pius VIII, Gregory XVI, Pius IX and Leo XIII have condemned Freemasonry and its principles. Both the 1917 (art. 2335) and 1983 (art. 1374) Code of Canon Law have imposed the penalties of excommunication and interdict on Catholics who become Freemasons. One must bear in mind that most newcomers to Freemasonry are for the most part oblivious to the ultimate goal of the society. In his encyclical *Humanum Genus* Pope Leo XII stated that the unsuspecting newcomers to the secret society are most likely unaware of their ultimate goals and should not be considered partners in the criminal acts perpetrated by Freemasonry.

However, after the Vatican II Council some clerics questioned the church's condemnation of Freemasonry because the 1983 code condemned all ties with "an association which plots against the church," without specific mention of Freemasonry. Because the revised code of canon law is not explicit on this point, some drew the mistaken conclusion that the Church's prohibition of Freemasonry had been dropped. As a result of this confusion, shortly before the 1983 code was promulgated, the Sacred

Congregation for the Doctrine of the Faith issued a statement indicating that the penalty was still in force. This statement was dated November 26, 1983 and may be found in *Origins* 13/27 (Nov. 15, 1983), 450. This statement from the Vatican's Doctrinal Congregation reads as follows:

> The question has been raised whether the church's position on Masonic associations has been altered, especially since no explicit mention is made of them in the new Code of Canon Law, as there was in the old code. This sacred congregation is able to reply that the circumstance is to be attributed to a criterion adopted in drafting. This criterion was observed also in regard to other associations which were likewise passed over in silence, because they were included in broader categories. *The church's negative position on Masonic associations therefore remains unaltered,* since their principles have always been regarded as irreconcilable with the church's doctrine. Hence joining them remains prohibited by the church. *Catholics enrolled in Masonic associations are involved in serious sin and may not approach Holy Communion.* Local ecclesiastical authorities do not have the faculty to pronounce a diminution of the above-mentioned judgment, in accordance with the intention of this congregation's declaration delivered Feb. 17, 1981.[87]

The former supreme pontiff John Paul II approved the above declaration February 17, 1981, deliberated at an ordinary meeting, and this declaration was signed by Cardinal Joseph Ratzinger (Pope Benedict XVI), and Archbishop Jerome Hamer, OP, secretary.

The forces of Communism and Freemasonry are closely linked to the two beasts in Antichrist's ascension to power. In the words of Pope

---

[87] AAS 73 [1981] pp. 240-241.

Pius XI, the rapid diffusion of the communistic ideas has seeped into every avenue and vein of Christian society, through the aid of the press and media largely controlled by the occult forces, including Freemasonry.[88] St. John reveals that the first beast "was mortally wounded, but this mortal wound was healed." When posited in the context of the aforesaid operations of Communism and Freemasonry, a correlation emerges between the two beasts and the atheistic forces. Freemasonry extends to Communism what Communism is incapable of achieving, and that is a more efficient way to subject the world to its atheistic ideas. Communism works from without while Freemasonry works from within many Christian and philanthropic organizations. By this means, Freemasonry effectively eviscerates the morale, doctrine, customs and tradition of veteran churches and religious based organizations.

The secret society of Freemasonry and its world-wide organizations engaged in ceaseless war against the Church was beheld in mystical vision by Blessed Anne Catherine Emmerich. Blessed Catherine's ignorance of the Book of Revelation – she had very little knowledge of Scripture – renders the vision of the first beast of the sea, revealed to her by her angel, all the more convincing:

> I see new martyrs, not of the present but of the future... I saw the *secret society*[89] undermining the great Church (St. Peter's) and near them a horrible beast that arose out of the sea. It had a tail like a fish, claws like a lion, and numberless heads that lay like a crown around one large head; its jaws were large and red, its body spotted like a tiger. It was very familiar with the demolishers (of the Church)... I saw the demolishers thronging into it accompanied by the beast... St. Peter's was almost entirely destroyed by the

---

[88]   *Divini Redemptoris*, Pope Pius XI, Encyclical Letter on Atheistic Communism promulgated on March 19, 1937, nn. 17, 18, 59.

[89]   Throughout her visions Blessed Emmerich specifically mentions the "Illuminati" and the "Freemasons" as secret societies most dangerous to the Catholic Church.

sect... I fear that the Holy Father will suffer
many tribulations before his death, for I see the
black counterfeit church gaining ground, I see its
fatal influence on the public.[90]

4.1.7 Miracle

In contrast to the forces of evil, several contemporary revelations
prophesy a great sign that will restore to the world much needed hope.
They predict a great miracle and a permanent sign in the sky after the
Warning. Although no approved revelation has revealed in exact detail
the great miracle or sign in the sky, several seers have affirmed that the
great miracle will take place in one geographical location, yet the graces
that will radiate from it will cover the entire earth for the purpose of
converting the world. It will be seen so clearly that no one will doubt that
it comes from God. It is also reported that the sick that come to the site of
the miracle on that day will be cured.

If the great miracle is a phenomenon that only a few seers have
seen and revealed in part only, approved private revelations intimate
its world-wide effects shortly before the chastisement. St. Hildegard
affirms:

> At this time, as a punishment for their sins...a
> powerful wind will rise in the north carrying
> heavy fog and the densest cloud of dust by
> divine command, and it will rage against them
> [the persecutors of the Christians] and it will fill
> their throats and eyes so that they cease savagery
> and be stricken with great amazement. Then
> within the Christian people *the holy Godhead will
> accomplish signs and wonders as it accomplished
> them at the time of Moses with the pillar of cloud
> and as Michael the Archangel did when he fought
> the heathen for the sake of Christians.*[91]

---

[90] Emmerich, vol. II, pp.290-292.

[91] St. Hildegard, 12th Century, Divinum Operorum, St. Hildegardis, Heading 24, in

Blessed Catherine Emmerich beheld with greater clarity a great sign in the sky:

> When the angel had descended I beheld above him a great shining cross in the heavens. On it hung the Savior from whose Wounds shot brilliant rays over the whole earth. Those glorious wounds were red... their center goldyellow... He wore no crown of thorns, but from all the Wounds of His Head streamed rays. Those from His Hands, Feet, and Side were fine as hair shone with rainbow colors; sometimes they were all united and fell upon villages, cities, and houses throughout the world... I also saw a shining red heart floating in the air. From one side flowed a current of white light to the Wound of the Sacred Side, and from the other a second current fell upon the Church in many regions; its rays attracted numerous souls who, by the Heart and the current of light, entered into the Side of Jesus. I was told that this was the Heart of Mary. Beside these rays, I saw from all the Wounds about thirty ladders let down to earth.[92]

Jesus revealed to the Servant of God Marthe Robin (1902-1981 A.D.) a sign of the two hearts like the one seen by Blessed Emmerich. Jesus tells Marthe:

> I play with the plans of men. My right hand prepares miracles and My Name shall be glorified in all the world. I shall be pleased to break the pride of the wicked... and much more admirable and extraordinary will be "the event" that will come out of our encounter... two glorious

---

Catholic Prophecy, Ibid., p. 16.

[92] Emmerich, Ibid., Vol. I, pp. 567-568.

thrones will arise, one of My sacred Heart and
the other of the Immaculate Heart of Mary.

St. Faustina Kowalska had a vision identical to the one witnessed by
Blessed Emmerich:

> Before I come as the just judge, I am coming first
> as the King of Mercy. Before the day of justice
> arrives, there will be given to people a sign in the
> heavens of this sort: All light in the heavens will
> be extinguished, and there will be great darkness
> over the whole earth. *Then the sign of the cross will
> be seen in the sky, and from the openings where the
> hands and the feet of the Savior were nailed will
> come forth great lights which will light up the earth
> for a period of time.*[93]

In the approved revelations of Betania, Venezuela, Maria Esperanza
reveals:

> Pretty soon Our Lord is going to give us a test,
> but it is a good test. It is not a bad test, and *most
> of us are going to see Him*, to see this event, and it
> is beautiful… It's not going to be the end, and its
> going to happen pretty soon. It's going to renew us
> completely… He is coming – not the end of the
> world, but the end of this century's agony. This
> century is purifying, and after will come peace and
> love. That's why our Mother has come to reconcile
> us. With reconciliation will come peace.[94]

4.1.8   The Comet

Many modern prophecies have consistently foretold a chastisement
if, after the great miracle, people do not turn back to God. All the more

---

[93]   St. Maria Faustina, *Diary of Divine Mercy*, entry 83.

[94]   Maria Esperanza to Michael Brown, in the book, *The Bridge to Heaven*, Spirit Daily
Pub., 1993

startling are the ancient and modern prophecies of the impact of an asteroid and its effects. Today's scientists confirm that a comet may enter the earth's path at any given moment. They also confirm that a comet encounter with the earth's atmosphere is more than sufficient to wipe out all traces of life on our planet. In the 12th century St. Hildegard foresaw a comet event before the Era of Peace:

> A powerful wind will rise in the north carrying heavy fog and the densest of dust by divine command, and it will fill their throats and eyes so that they will cease their savagery and be stricken with a great fear. Before *the comet* comes, many nations, the good excepted, will be scourged by want and famine… By its tremendous pressure the comet will force much out of the ocean and flood many countries, causing much want and many plagues. All coastal cities will live in fear, and many of them will be destroyed by tidal waves, and most living creatures will be killed, even those who escape from horrible diseases. For in none of those cities does a person live according to the laws of God.[95]

> Peace will return to the world when the white flower again takes possession of the throne of France.[96] During this period of peace, people will be forbidden to carry weapons, and iron will be used only for making agricultural implements and tools. Also during this period, the land will be very productive, and many Jews, heathens and heretics will join the Church.[97]

[95] St. Hildegard, 12th Century, *Divinum Operorum*, St. Hildegardis, Heading 24.

[96] The "white flower" is the symbol of the great monarchy, the Lily whom I refer to below.

[97] St. Hildegard, in *Catholic Prophecy*, p.16.

Earlier I cited prophecies concerning a chastisement from man in the form of wars if humankind does not repent. Blessed Anna-Maria Taigi beheld another, far more ferocious chastisement that will come directly from Heaven:

> God will send two punishments: one will be in the form of wars, revolutions and other evils; it shall originate on earth. The other will be sent from Heaven.[98]

In Akita, Japan the Blessed Virgin Mary implored conversion and repentance in reparation for sin to offset the chastisement from Heaven:

> As I told you, if men do not repent and better themselves, the Father will inflict a terrible punishment on all humanity. It will be a punishment greater than the deluge, such as one will never seen before. Fire will fall from the sky and will wipe out a great part of humanity, the good as well as the bad, sparing neither priests nor faithful. The survivors will find themselves so desolate that they will envy the dead. The only arms which will remain for you will be the Rosary and the Sign left by My Son. Each day recite the prayers of the Rosary. With the Rosary, pray for the Pope, the bishops and priests.
>
> The work of the devil will infiltrate even into the Church in such a way that one will see cardinals opposing cardinals, bishops against bishops. The priests who venerate me will be scorned and opposed by their confreres...churches and altars sacked; the Church will be full of those who accept compromises and the demon will press many priests and consecrated souls to leave the service of the Lord.

---

[98] Blessed Anna Maria Taigi, in Catholic Prophecy, p.44.

The demon will be especially implacable against
souls consecrated to God. The thought of the
loss of so many souls is the cause of my sadness.
If sins increase in number and gravity, there will
be no longer pardon for them.[99]

The prophetic analyst Yves Dupont reports that a comet encounter
with the earth is indeed possible. Comets are low-density fiery bodies in
space that are made up of a head, hair and a tail. The hair is formed of
gases that emit a bright light. The tail always remains in the direction
of the sun, and not necessarily behind the comet. When the comet's tail
crosses a planet's path its remnants crash to the ground. These remnants
may range from fine dust to coarse ash, from gravel to boulders. Since
the comet's atmosphere is sometimes composed of methane it may indeed
ignite and poison the earth's atmosphere. This does not mean the complete
annihilation of human life, but as reported in the Book of Zechariah and
in approved private revelations, it may signify a purification of the earth's
elements by fire in which two thirds of the human race will perish and one
third remain. The effects of a comet approaching the earth may certainly
explain the Akita and Cuapa prophecies of fire in the sky.

Blessed Elizabeth Canori-Mora describes one of the chastisements
that may result from the gaseous, atmospheric conditions of an asteroid:

The sky was covered with clouds so dense and
dismal that it was impossible to look at them
without dismay. All of the sudden there burst
out such a terrible and violent wind, that its
noise sounded like the roars of furious lions. The
sound of the furious hurricane was heard over
the whole earth. Fear and terror struck not only
men, but the very beasts.[100]

---

[99] *Call of Ages*, Ibid., p. 375. Message of October 13, 1973.

[100] St. Elizabeth Canori-Mora, in *The Christian Trumpet*, Ibid., p.180. It appears that
immediately before the three days' darkness a violent global hurricane will purify the
earth of its former polluted and iniquitous airs, transforming it into an Eden-like
dwelling place for the Sabbatine remnant.

It is possible that the earth's oxygen will ignite the hydrogen of the comet's tail, resulting in devastating hurricanes. The oxygen supply that is consumed by the raging fires in various parts of the sky will, in turn, cause people who leave their homes or shelters to die from asphyxiation. Hence the recent prophecies exhorting us during the darkness to "stay indoors; keep your windows shut."[101]

4.1.9   Three Days of Darkness

If the ensuing dust to coarse ash from the comet's tail enters the earth's atmosphere it will invariably darken it by inhibiting the sun's light and heat and causing a drop in temperatures. We discover a biblical parallel to this phenomenon in the Book of Exodus:

> And the Lord said to Moses: Stretch out thy hands toward heaven: and may there be darkness upon the land of Egypt, so thick that it may be felt. And Moses stretched forth his hand towards heaven, *and there came horrible darkness in all, the land of Egypt for three days.* No man saw his brother, nor moved himself out of the place where he was; but whatsoever the children of Israel dwelt there was light.[102]

The Book of Joel reads:

> And I will show wonders in heaven: in the earth blood and fire and vapor of smoke. The sun shall be turned into darkness and the moon into blood.[103]

---

[101]   Albert J. Hebert, *The Three Day's Darkness*, P.O. Box 309, Paulina, Press, LA 1986, p. XI.

[102]   Ex 10:21-23.

[103]   Joel 3:4.

The Book of Acts reveals:

> It will come to pass in the last days, God says, that I will pour out a portion of my spirit upon all flesh... I will work wonders in the heavens above and signs in the earth below; blood, fire and a cloud of smoke. The sun shall be turned into darkness, and the moon to blood, before the coming of the great and splendid day of the Lord, and it shall be that everyone shall be saved who calls on the name of the Lord.[104]

One of the comet's devastating effects that numerous visionaries foretell is the three days of darkness. The 19th century Blessed Sister Mary of Jesus Crucified writes:

> *During a darkness lasting three days* the people given to evil will perish so that only *one fourth of mankind will survive.*[105]

Another 19th century Blessed Caspar del Bufalo adds:

> The death of the impenitent persecutors of the Church will take place during the three days of darkness.[106]

The earth's darkness is a biblical event that is traceable to the Books of Exodus and Revelation. Worthy of mention are the accompanying chastisements foretold in the Book of Revelation. Here one is introduced to the *six seals* (Rev. 6), the *seven trumpets* (Rev. 8-11) and the *seven bowls* (Rev. 15.5-16) that precede, accompany and follow the earth's darkness.

---

[104] Acts 2:17. 19-21.

[105] *Three Days' Darkness*, Ibid., p. 20.

[106] Blessed Caspar del Bufalo, *Catholic Prophecy*, Ibid., p.79.

4.1.10 Seven Seals

In light of the aforestated events, the seven seals of the Book of Revelation appear to unfold as follows: If people do not heed *the Warning* of Christ (first seal), there will ensue a great war at the hands of men [World War III], causing much bloodshed (second seal). This will be a chastisement from man, not from God. Many revolutions, civil and global wars, and natual disasters will claim the lives of many people and cause food to become so scarce that a famine will follow resulting in the death of millions of people. Their unburied bodies will cause worldwide pestilence and epidemics. As a result many will suffer from famine and want (third seal). One quarter of the human race will eventually perish from the war, and from its ensuing famine and plagues (fourth seal). Those that had been martyred during this period will intercede before God's throne (fifth seal).

In order to save mankind from self-annihilation God will send from the heavens a chastisement in the form of a comet. Yves Dupont reports that when the tail of the Exodus comet crossed the path of the earth, a red dust, impalpable, like fine flour fell. It was too fine to be seen, and for this reason it is not mentioned in Exodus 7.21, yet it colored everything red, and the waters of the Egyptians turned to blood. Also the comet's tail brought a coarser dust, like ash that is recorded in Exodus 10:23, which plunged the world into darkness for three days. This coarse ash irritated the skin and eyes of those that were outside, so much so that it is likely that they scratched their eyes and skin thus creating sores and boils, which, for want of being treated, turned into pustules. Soon the infection spread throughout their entire bodies and death followed. Likewise the comet that God will send will leave in its wake an ash-like substance that will obscure the light of the sun, thereby causing the sun to turn black, the moon to turn blood red, and the stars to disappear from the sky. A great earthquake will result, possibly from the gravitational pull of the comet's head, every mountain and island will be shaken, and all will attempt to hide themselves in caves (sixth seal). Natural laws would indicate that the great earthquake will be followed by a great silence (seventh seal).

Worthy of mention are the ancient documents (an Egyptian papyrus, a Mexican manuscript, parchments from Finland, India, etc.)

that report a crossing comet more than 3,000 years ago, around the time of Exodus, that caused a redness of blood in the waters and over the moon: *Non igneo sed sanguineo rubore fuisse* ("It was not the redness of fire, but the redness of blood").[107] It is also likely that soon after the fine and coarse ash, there will cascade into the earth's atmosphere particles from the comet and asteroids in progressively larger sizes: gravel, stones and even boulders. Hence the seven trumpets.

4.1.11 Seven Trumpets

From a scientific angle, the *seven trumpets* appear more akin to what we now call a meteor shower. Thus we read in the Book of Revelation the devastating effects with each trumpet that closely resemble the effects of such a shower: Hail and fire mixed with blood are hurled down to earth burning up one third of the land, trees and grass (first trumpet). Something like a large burning mountain is hurled into the sea, and a third of all creatures in the sea die and a third of the ships are wrecked (second trumpet). A large star burning like a torch falls from the sky onto a third of the rivers and springs. It is called wormwood, and a third of all water turned into wormwood, and many died (third trumpet). A third of the sun, moon and stars grow dark, the day and night lose light for a third of the time (fourth trumpet). A star falls to the earth, which opens the passage to the abyss: Smoke comes out and causes the sun and air to be darkened. Locusts torment for five months those who do not have the seal of God (fifth trumpet). One third of the human race perishes by the effects of fire, smoke, sulfur: the effects of the gaseous, atmospheric conditions of a meteor shower (sixth trumpet). Lightning, thunder, rumblings and a violent hailstorm ensue (seventh trumpet).

4.1.12 Seven Bowls

With respect to the *seven bowls,* we discover that those who received the mark of the beast will be stricken with the festering, ugly sores caused by coarse-comet ash (first bowl). The red ash particles

---

[107] *Catholic Prophecy,* Yves Dupont, p.84.

from the comet then cause the seas to turn to blood and every living sea
creature to die (second bowl; intensification of the second trumpet). The
rivers and springs turn to blood also (third bowl; intensification of the
third trumpet). The sun's heat, intensified by the methane gas from the
comet's atmosphere, burns people with fire, but they do not repent (fourth
bowl). The throne of the beast and his kingdom are plunged into darkness
due to the dust-like ash of the comet's tail (fifth bowl; intensification of
the fourth trumpet). The Euphrates river is dried up for the kings of the
East to pass, and they assemble in Armageddon (sixth trumpet). There is
lightning, thunder, rumblings and a violent hailstorm (seventh trumpet),
and every mountain and island is moved (seventh bowl; intensification of
the sixth seal).

Given the foregoing, the six seals, the seven trumpets and the
seven bowls emerge as a series of punishments that are associated with
the chastisement *before* the Era of Peace. Still, they ought not be
limited to that period only. Biblical parallels demonstrate that in history
each manifestation of evil is followed by an intensification of evil patterned
after the preceding manifestation. So if in the days of Exodus we find
darkness, plagues, famine and death, so in the Book of Revelation do we
encounter similar events shortly before *and* after the Era of Peace though
on a much larger scale. Simply put, the woes that follow the Era of Peace
will resemble and, in some instances, surpass the woes that preceded it.

Between the seven trumpets and seven bowls two mysterious
figures emerge. The Book of Revelation presents "two witnesses" that are
sent by God to turn peoples hearts back to him and to refute Antichrist.
The names of these two witnesses remain hidden, yet some mystics have
identified them in the spiritual sense as the Sacred and Immaculate
Hearts of Jesus and Mary, or as Elijah and Moses who have come back to
earth. Early Church Tradition identifies these two witnesses as Enoch and
Elias. St. Hippolytus, Tertullian, Ss. Basil the Great, John Damascene
(675-749 A.D.), Hildegarde and Blessed Catherine Emmerich refer to
the two witnesses of the Book of Revelation as Enoch and Elijah. For
purposes of brevity I recall four texts:

St. Hippolytus:

> For when the threescore and two weeks are
> fulfilled, and Christ is come, and the Gospel is
> preached in every place, the times being then
> accomplished, there will remain only one week,
> the last, in which *Elias will appear, and Enoch,*
> *and in the midst of it the abomination of desolation*
> *will be manifested,* viz., Antichrist, announcing
> desolation to the world.[108]

Tertullian:

> Enoch no doubt was translated, and so was
> Elijah; nor did they experience death: it was
> postponed, (and only postponed), most certainly:
> *they are reserved for the suffering of death, that by*
> *their blood they may extinguish Antichrist.*[109]

Blessed Emmerich relates a mystical vision in which she saw
Elijah, who was taken up to paradise in a fiery chariot to prepare for the
day of Antichrist:

> Last night I journeyed… to a region of incredible
> beauty… Numbers of animals sported around
> apparently harmless… From this paradise I
> mounted still higher, as if through the clouds,
> and at last, came to the summit of the mountain,
> where I saw wonders… A manly, holy, shining
> figure sitting cross-legged in eastern fashion, and
> writing with a reed on a large roll of parchment…
> I saw standing a single chariot with four low
> wheels… The man who sits at the table will come
> in due time. His chariot remains as a perpetual
> memorial. *He mounted up there in it and men, to*

---

[108] Hippolytus, *The Fathers of the Church*, Ibid., On Daniel, Part II, 22.

[109] Tertullian, Ibid., The Soul's Testimony, Ch. L.

their astonishment, will behold him coming again in the same. I returned by a narrow descending path and saw the Mountain of the Prophets, on which everything seemed even more flourishing than usual. There were two figures occupied under the tent... Paradise is not far from this mountain. Once before I saw that Elijah lived in a garden near Paradise.[110]

Also St. Hildegarde affirms that "Enoch and Elias are in paradise," not in the heavenly courts proper to the saints and angels, but in the paradisiacal garden that Adam and Eve left unspoiled and awaiting the day when God will call upon them to refute Antichrist.[111]

Irrespective of their identity, the two witnesses will return to earth to prophesy in the name of God, to turn peoples' hearts to him and to refute Antichrist whose kingdom God may chastise with a comet. Despite the devastating effects of foretold the comet that will claim far more lives than the preceding world war, its consequential hurricanes will quickly replenish oxygen, thereby foreshortening the days of chastisement. Hurricanes of heavy winds and dense clouds may cause torrential rains that will, in turn, quench the many fires on earth and cause flooding. These floods will then fecundate and rejuvenate the earth's soil. The hurricanes and rains can also disperse the infected air once laden with the pestilence and epidemics of many unburied bodies that the remaining one third will bury. After the comet's dust, lightning and hurricanes have purified the air, the land will yield abundantly during the Era of Peace. Because the ash and dust from the comet's tail are very rich in minerals and have fertilizing properties, their precipitation will help restore the proper balance of the atmosphere. The binding of large quantities of oxygen causes asphyxiation, yet lightning precipitates nitrogen of the air into the earth's soil as a fertilizing agent, as all plants need nitrogen, but only few can absorb it directly from the air.

---

[110]   Ibid., vol. I, pp. 556-564.

[111]   Emmerich, Ibid., vol. I, p. 155.

Modern technology and science allows us to better apprehend the nature of the pending chastisement. While the combined effects of the two chastisements from man and from God, from the third World War and from the comet, may wipe out two thirds of the human race, it will leave the remaining one third to repopulate the earth throughout the Era of Peace. During this period humanity will return to a simple, agrarian life, tilling the land from which it came. Because man in his desire to better the earth has taken from it without replenishing it, and has managed to disfigure it to the point of extinction, God will reawaken within him the first impulse of love for the earth from which he came. Man was created for God through his relation to the earth, to its creatures and the cosmos. Thus the more he learns to respect the world around him, the more its resources and potencies are available to him in his service to God and to all creatures. Once man grasps this fundamental truth, God opens his eyes to a reality that stood before him in the days of Adam, where he beholds the Creator's handiwork in every creature, where he cultivates and shepherds the earth as God intended, and where he gives back to the earth for that which he received. Indeed it is in gaining respect for the earth that man gains respect for all life around him. For God fashioned nature in such a way that it takes very good care of man, it provides for him both physically and spiritually, and by its example, trains him to care for all other creatures.

4.1.13 Divine Assistance

Although Antichrist and his black church will have their hour, in the end God will triumph. St. Thomas Aquinas teaches that during the reign of Antichrist God will not cease to assist his creatures, as he will prevent Satan from harming us as he pleases by limiting Satan's power:

> Infidels and even Antichrist are not deprived... of the guardianship of angels. Although this help... does not result in... eternal life by good works, it does nonetheless... protect them from certain evils which would hurt themselves and others. *Even the demons are checked by good angels lest they harm as much as they would. In like*

manner Antichrist will not do as much harm as he
would wish.[112]

St. Margaret Mary Alacoque (1647-1690 A.D.) reveals that the
purpose of devotion to the Sacred Heart in these latter days is to assist
us:

> I understood that devotion to the Sacred Heart
> is a last effort of His Love towards Christians
> of these latter times, by proposing to them an
> object and means so calculated to persuade them
> to love Him.[113]

Our Lady reveals to St. Catherine Labouré (1806-1876 A.D.) the
protection and aid we receive from the miraculous medal:

> God wishes to charge you with a mission. You
> will be contradicted, but do not fear; you will
> have the grace to do what is necessary. Tell
> your spiritual director all that passes within
> you. Times are evil... The entire world will be
> distressed with afflictions... Come to the foot of
> the altar. Graces will be shed on all, great and
> little, especially upon those who seek for them...
> There will be much persecution. The cross will
> be treated with contempt. It will be hurled to
> the ground and blood will flow... *Have a medal*
> *struck as I have shown you. All who wear it will*
> *receive great graces.* (When Catherine received
> her share of these first medals from the hands of
> her spiritual director Father Jean Marie Aladel,
> Mary said): Now it must be propagated.[114]

---

[112] *Summa Theologica*, Thomas Aquinas, Part I, Q. 113, Art. 4, Benzinger Bros. New
York 1947.

[113] www.kurescek.info/sacred-heart-the-nine-first-fridaydevotion.html. Imprimatur: E.
Morrogh Bernard. Vic. Gen., Westmonasterii, 1954.

[114] Our Lady of the Rosary Library Prospect, KY Website: www.olrl.org/lives/

Jesus and Mary often reveal the efficacy of the Church's Sacraments, sacramentals and devotions that communicate to people a supernatural and divine protection from God. Among the Sacraments the greatest of all is the Eucharist, as it is God himself. That the Blessed Sacrament will be especially powerful in the days of tribulation and darkness is made clear in the writings of Blessed Catherine Emmerich:

> The Blessed Sacrament had the appearance of a little luminous, transparent Infant in the center of a resplendent sun, surrounded by myriads of angels and saints in great splendor and magnificence. It is inexpressible! ... This was not the historic scene (of the Last Supper)... *It represented the Blessed Sacrament in time of persecution*... I saw the Feast of Corpus Christi ... I saw the feast celebrated by numbers of early Christians, by those of our times, and by many belonging to the future.[115]

All God-fearing people will experience God's divine intervention during the reign of Antichrist. God's divine protection will lend itself in difficult times especially through the following Sacraments:

- *Baptism* cleanses the soul of original sin and infuses within it the gifts of faith, hope and love.
- *Confession* washes the soul clean of all past mortal and venial sins, sanctifies and strengthens it, and enlightens the intellect to better apprehend the will of God.
- *Communion (the Eucharist)*, when received in the state of grace, becomes the greatest source of protection against the snares of the devil.

---

[115] Emmerich, vol. II, p. 140-141. Blessed Emmerich's speaks of a "feast celebrated by numbers of early Christians, by those of our times, and by many belonging to the future." Here she appears to allude to the martyred of the First Resurrection of Rev:19 (whom Lactantius identifies as "the just that have lived from the beginning") who will "appear" to the remnant survivors throughout the Era of Peace.

Among the sacramentals that dispose us to receive God's power and protection, the following are especially efficacious:

+ Brown Scapular
+ Holy Water
+ Benedictine Medal
+ Miraculous Medal
+ Crucifix
+ Enthronement and Blessing of Homes

The following Church devotions increase our virtues to enable us to face trials with greater trust and an upright intention:

+ Eucharistic Adoration
+ Daily participation in the Holy Sacrifice of the Mass
+ Rosary
+ Chaplet of Divine Mercy
+ First Nine Fridays of the month (requested by Jesus to St. Margaret Mary Alacoque)
+ First Five Saturdays of the month (requested by the Blessed Virgin Mary of Fatima)
+ Meditation on The Hours of the Passion (requested by Jesus to the Servant of God Luisa Piccarreta)
+ Stations of the Cross
+ Consecration Prayers to Jesus, Mary and Joseph
+ Guardian Angel Entrustment Prayer

4.1.14 Minor Judgment

In the Nicene Creed the Church teaches that when Christ returns for the second time in the flesh, "he will come as judge of the living and the dead" ("*venturus est judicare vivos et mortuos*").[116] This

---

[116] The classical creeds of the Church are popularly known as the Apostle's Creed and the Creed of Nicea-Constantinople. Two other creeds that merit our attention are the Athanasian Creed and the Creed of Pius IV. The popular Apostle's Creed reflects the teaching of the Apostles but is not of apostolic origin. This creed, popular to all Christian confessional Churches of the West, traditionally dates as far back

event, commonly referred to as the Day of the Lord, is called the Final or General Judgment. It is *final* because there are no judgments that follow, and *general* because it is a public sentence pronounced on all souls rejoined to their resurrected bodies. At the General Judgment, not only will there take place the judgment in the body of all believers *and* nonbelievers, but also a theodicy—a justification of God in the sight of all creatures; it is God's final act of judging, which is at once Christ's Second Coming in the flesh and the cause of mankind's resurrection.[117] This does not, however, preclude the possibility of an antecedent Particular Judgment of nonbelievers who follow the spirit of Antichrist. Indeed Noah and his family, the remnant survivors of a wicked generation, experienced a Particular Judgment of this sort. God's sentence on Noah's generation was directed toward *all* nonbelievers dead to God's grace though physically alive, yet it was neither final nor general.

The Early Ecclesiastical Writers Lactantius, Hippolytus and Tertullian unequivocally place the future, Particular Judgment of the martyrs and all nonbelievers *before* the Era of Peace. And approved writings of Church saints and mystics affirm that a Particular Judgment will indeed occur during an antichristian world-rebellion. It has been called by the German stigmatist Teresa Neumann a future "minor judgment." She stated that *"Our Lord himself called it a minor judgment."*[118]

St. John Vianney confirms Teresa's words:

> The communists of Paris, after their defeat, shall
> spread themselves through all France, and will be

as the second century, and was a rudimentary formula professed by catechumens before the reception of Baptism. The Nicene Creed (Creed of Nicea-Constantinople) is a composition of elements of doctrine contained in an early baptismal creed of Jerusalem, as well as enactments of the Councils of Nicea (325) and Constantinople (381). It is more extensive than the Apostle's creed and has become, since the fifth century, the only creed used in liturgies in the East and from the eighth century, in the liturgies of the West.

[117] J.H. Wright, "Judgment", *The New Catholic Encyclopedia*, Ibid., VIII, 30ff.

[118] *Call of Ages*, Ibid., p. 183.

greatly multiplied... A civil war shall break out everywhere. These wicked people shall become masters in the North, East and Southwest of France. They will imprison very many persons, and will be guilty of more massacres. They will attempt to kill all priests and all the religious. But this shall not last long. People will imagine that all is lost; but the good God shall save all. *It will be like a sign of the last judgment... Religion shall flourish again better than ever before.*[119]

Scripture reveals that two thirds of humanity will experience a Particular Judgment during the chastisement. We read in the Book of Zechariah:

In all the land, says the Lord, *two thirds of them shall be cut off and perish, and one third shall be left.* I will bring on third through fire, and I will refine them as silver is refined, and I will test them as gold is tested. They shall call upon my name, and I will hear them.[120]

And Venerable Bartholomew Holzhauser states that few will remain on earth to inherit the Era of Peace:

Those who survive the sword, plague and famines, will be few on earth.[121]

---

[119] St. John Vianney, in *The Christian Trumpet*, Ibid., pp.87-88.

[120] Zec. 13:8-9.

[121] Venerable Bartholomew Holzhauser, *Catholic Prophecy*, Ibid., p.38.

CHAPTER 5

THE WOMAN AND THE DRAGON

Since Satan is bent on aping God's plan of salvation, one of the many weapons he employs in its destruction is the woman. Statistics show that there are far more cases of diabolical possession with woman than with men. The reason? Satan seeks to counter the *Proto-evangelium*. The *Proto-evangelium* is the first announcement of salvation, the first foretelling of victory over evil. In Gn. 3:15 we read, "I will put enmity between you and the woman, and between your offspring and hers; He will strike at your head while you strike at his heel." Pope John Paul II states, "She [the woman] is assigned the first place in the Proto-evangelium as the progenitrix of him who will be the Redeemer of man."[122] In view of Mary and her future triumph, Satan becomes enraged and seeks to avenge himself upon all women.

Father Gabriel Amorth, the exorcist of the Archdiocese of Rome – whom I had the privilege of assisting as associate exorcist – made the following statement:

> It is above all women who are stricken by the demonic because they are more easily exposed than men to the danger of the demonic... I have encountered numerous cases of woman who, because of demonic possession, were forced to prostitute themselves. For this reason, they have no moral blame... The woman preyed upon by Satan are especially those who are young and of

---

[122] Pope John Paul II, *The Theology of the Body*, Pauline Books & Media, Boston 1997, p.458.

pleasing appearance... During some exorcisms,
the demon, with a terrifying voice, has roared
that he seeks to enter woman rather than men
in order to take revenge on Mary because he has
been humiliated by her.[123]

If Satan targets women, it is because Mary, the Ark that bore the
Redeemer, possesses an efficacious power that far exceeds that of other
creatures. Her total abandonment to God's will released, as it were, the
reservoirs of his grace, whereby Scripture extols her as the woman "full
of grace." And Mary, being the new Eve and Mother of the Church in the
new order of grace, communicates to her children the graces God imparts
to her.

As the Ark that bore the divine Redeemer, Mary participated in
the mission of Redemption. Because she gave birth and sustenance to the
divine Redeemer, Satan's contempt for her is unbounded. Satan did all in
his power to dissuade Mary from carrying out the plan of Redemption
beside her divine Son: She would be forced to make an arduous journey to
Egypt; experience rejection at an inn in her time of expectancy; receive into
her arms the lifeless body of her Son, and endure many years of solitude
and separation from the One who gave life its meaning. Satan caused
Mary immense sufferings in order to dissuade her from standing by the
Cross of Redemption and from carrying out her role as co-redemptrix.[124]
Yet Satan's plans were permitted and even used by God for humankind's
sanctification and salvation, for God knows how to convert even evil to
good. Having been spectator to Mary's unwavering fidelity to the Will of
God in the work of Redemption, and realizing that his plans against the
woman prophesied in Genesis had failed, Satan then sought to obtain

---

[123] *Inside the Vatican*, article by Amorth, Fr. Gabriel, January 1994 edition, Rome,
Italy.

[124] "Mary's role in the Church is inseparable from her union with Christ and flows
directly from it. 'This union of the mother and the Son in the work of salvation is
made manifest from the time of Christ's virginal conception up to his death'" (CCC,
Ibid., 946); "In a wholly and singular way she cooperated... in the Savior's work of
restoring supernatural life of souls" (Ibid., 968).

what satisfaction he could by snatching souls from God through other women. In this way the exorcist of Rome affirms that Satan uses certain women, that is, until the Woman and her seed will crush his head.

If Satan has marked women, God has done so even more for his universal plan of Redemption. If the majority of prophets in the Old Testament were men, from the twelfth century onwards proclaiming the prophetic word of God became more and more a female privilege. God raised up many women to whom he communicated direct prophetic revelations with innumerable messages for the Church. Among these prophets who occupied a very active role in the society of their time, worthy of mention are Ss. Bridget of Sweden and Catherine of Sienna. Other mystics of the last century include the Servant of God Luisa Piccarreta, Maria Valtorta and Marthe Robin, who lived completely secluded lives, compelled by chronic illness. The writings of these women became known through the activities of their confessors, and through the interest of ordinary believers whose lives had been changed by their writings. Many of these prophets share in the spirituality of the early Christian martyrs, for they considered their sufferings as a participation in the salvific paschal mission of Christ. God chose these spiritual female giants to help the Woman and her offspring crush the head of the serpent. They cooperated in Jesus' work of Redemption with Mary, who generated and formed them to do battle against the infernal serpent.

In one of the leading biblical journals composed by a theological commission, *Parola, Spirito e Vita*, a relationship is drawn between the Holy Spirit, Mary and her offspring.[125] Since Mary's maternity came by the power of the Holy Spirit for the purpose of generating and forming the Son of God, the Church bestows upon her the title "Mother of the Church" to illustrate the continuity of her mission of generating and forming other sons and daughters of God. St. Louis de Montfort (1673-1716 A.D.) reaffirms this prerogative of Mary in the end times:

---

[125] Aristide Serra, *Parola, Spirito e Vita*, semestrale—n.2, luglio—dicembre 1998/2, collana 38 Lo Spirito Santo (Centro editoriale dehoniano, Bologna, Italy); article *Lo Spirito Santo e Maria in Lc 1,35. Antico e Nuovo Testamento a confronto*, pp.119-140.

She [Mary] will consequently produce the
marvels which will be seen in the latter times.
*The formation and education of the great saints
who will come at the end of the world are reserved
to her.*[126]

Towards the end of the world... Almighty God
and his holy Mother are to raise up great saints
who will surpass in holiness most other saints as
much as the cedars of Lebanon tower above little
shrubs.[127]

In the second coming of Jesus Christ, Mary must
be known and openly revealed by the Holy Spirit
so that Jesus may be known, loved and served
through her.[128]

---

[126]   St. Louis de Monfort, in *Catholic Prophecy*, p.33.

[127]   St. Louis de Montfort, *True Devotion to Mary* (Rockford, IL: TAN Books, 1985),
Article 47, Ibid., n.25, p. 296.

[128]   Ibid., n.49, p.303. St. Louis' polyvalent expression "the second coming" reflects his
eschatology on an historic era of Christian holiness in which Christ reigns in the
souls of human creatures. St. Louis interprets Christ's second coming through his
Incarnation and his reign in Mary, through whom he extends his reign in other
creatures. He describes Mary's catalytic role in the rise of "the great saints" who
hasten the era of Christ's reign in souls. Montfort's "second coming" is understood
as an "interior" reign of Christ at a time of universal outpouring of grace and its
preparation by the action of the Spirit and Mary.
    When speaking of Christ's second coming, Montfort describes it in distinctly
interior and spiritual terms: Christ will reign in the souls of human creatures within
history. Although Monfort affirms that Christ's reign will be *spiritual* and *within*
human history, he also relates it to Christ's definitive and *physical* reign on earth
outside of human history, whereby Christ's second coming begins with his interior
reign in souls and culminates with his "exterior, physical and final" return in glory to
conclude human history.
    Montfort's thought may be summarized as follows: As Christ's "first coming"
embraces the Incarnation, his public life and the Cross, so his "second coming"
embraces his interior reign in souls (era of peace), his return in the flesh and the
final judgment (Parousia). The interior coming prepares the Church for the exterior
and final return of Jesus. Jesus came the first time "in self-abasement and privation,"

5.1   Triumph of the Immaculate Heart of Mary

Many mystics have referred to Mary as the prototype of Christian holiness throughout the Era of Peace. Mary's holiness will inspire Christians in the end times by virtue of her Immaculate Conception and perpetual fidelity to the Will of God, for these special gifts were given to her for the very purpose of generating God's children into the likeness of her divine Son. Her prerogative of generating sons into her divine Son draws its strength from her Son's holiness that is more purely reflected in her than in any other creature. St. Maximilian refers to Mary as the "Immaculata" to emphasize this truth. The expression "Immaculata" accentuates the dignity of Mary's office as Mother of the Son of God, whose purity and eternal holiness that eclipsed her entire being, empowers her to continuously generate God's children into the holiness she received. Indeed Maximilian speaks of a future era when all Christians will approach the holiness of Mary more closely than ever before. It will be an era of the triumph of the Immaculata, or, in the words of our Lady of Fatima, "the Triumph of her Immaculate Heart." At Fatima our Lady revealed that her heart will triumph and the world will be given an Era of Peace:

> In the end, my Immaculate Heart will triumph.
> The Holy Father will consecrate Russia to me,
> and she will be converted, and an era of peace
> shall be granted to the world.[129]

---

whereas he will come the second time interiorly to "reign over all the earth" and externally "to judge the living and the dead," Montfort affirms. One cannot overemphasize the point that Montfort's interior reign of Christ occurs *within* human history, whereas his judgment of "the living and the dead," occurs *outside* of history. These are two distinct and critical points that define Montfort's thought, and the failure to distinguish them leads to heresy of millenarianism. (For more information on Montfort's thought, I refer you to the work entitled, *Jesus Living in Mary: Handbook of the Spirituality of St. Louis de Montfort*, (Bay Shore, NY: Montfort Publications, 1994).

[129] Thomas W. Petrisko, *The Fatima Prophecies*, St. Andrew's Productions, Steubenville Pike, PA 1998.

Mary's privileged role in the end times is reinforced in the writings of Venerable Mary of Agreda (1602-1665 A.D.) and Saint Louis de Montfort:

> It was revealed to me that through the intercession of the Mother of God all heresies will disappear. The victory over heresies has been reserved by Christ for his Blessed Mother... The power of Mary in the latter days will be very conspicuous. Mary will extend the reign of Christ over the heathens and the Muslims, and it will be a time of great joy when Mary is enthroned as Mistress and Queen of hearts.[130]

> The power of Mary over all the evil spirits will especially shine forth in the latter times, when Satan will lie in wait of her heel, that is, her humble servants and her poor children whom she will rouse to fight against him... they will be great and exalted before God in holiness. They will be superior to all creatures by their great zeal and so strongly will they be supported by divine assistance that, in union with Mary, they will crush the head of Satan with their heel, that is, their humility, and bring about victory to Jesus Christ.[131]

St. Maximilian Kolbe (1894-1941 A.D.) affirms:

> The image of the Immaculate will one day replace the large red star over the Kremlin, but only after a great and bloody trial.[132]

[130] Blessed Mary of Agreda, *Catholic Propecy*, Ibid., p.33.

[131] St. Louis de Montfort, *True Devotion to Mary*, Monfort Publications, New York 1995, n.54, p.305. St. Louis uses the expression 'the second coming' as Ss. Bernard and Cyril, that is, not a Final Coming in the flesh but a pneumatic, hidden coming. Unlike the events that signal the and of the world, this second coming is characterized by the preaching of Jesus Christ to all nations.

[132] St. Maximilian Kolbe, quoted in Albert J. Herbert, S.M., *Signs, Wonders and Response*, (LA: 1988), p.126.

5.2   Era of Peace and the Reign of the Divine Will

Following the tribulation of the Antichrist False Prophet, the testimony of the Fathers and the saints indicates a long period of world-wide peace and holiness. Ss. Justin Martyr and Irenaeus describe the Era of Peace as man's reconciliation with God and creation:

> Wolves and lambs shall feed together, and the lion shall eat like the ox, and the serpent shall eat earth like bread.[133]

> Creation, reborn and freed from bondage, will yield an abundance of food of all kinds from the heaven's dew and the fertility of the earth...[134]

The 17th century Venerable Bartholomew Holzhauser writes on the Era of Peace:

> When everything has been ruined by war, when Catholics are hard pressed by traitorous co-religionists and heretics, when the Church and her servants are denied their rights, the monarchies have been abolished and their rulers murdered... then the Hand of Almighty God will work a marvelous change, something apparently impossible according to human understanding.[135]

Blessed Catherine Emmerich relates:

> When the combat on earth was over... the cross [that appeared in the heavens] also vanished and in its place stood a tall, resplendent lady extending over it her mantle of golden rays... I

---

[133] St. Justin Martyr, *Dialogue with Trypho*, Ibid., pp. 277-278.

[134] *Adversus Haereses*, Ibid., IV, 38,1; 20,5.

[135] Yves, inter alia, cf. also Venerable Bartholomew Holzhauser, 17th century. *Apocalypsin*, Ven. Bartholomew Holzhauser, 1850, p.69.

felt the kingdom of God was near. I perceived a new splendor, a higher life in all nature, and a holy emotion in all mankind… Then I saw a great feast in St. Peter's which, after the victorious battle, shone like the sun. I saw numerous processions entering it. I saw a new pope, earnest and energetic. I saw before the feast began a great many bad bishops and pastors expelled by him… I saw the petition: "Lord, Thy Kingdom come," being verified.[136]

In the Church-recognized messages of La Salette, our Lady predicted that after the reign of Antichrist, religion will flourish everywhere:

Rome will lose the faith and become the seat of Antichrist. The demons of the air together with the Antichrist will perform great wonders on earth and in the atmosphere, and men will become more and more perverted. God will take care of his faithful servants and men of good will. *The gospel will be preached everywhere, and all peoples of all nations will get to know the truth.*[137]

As indicated earlier, the approved writings of the saints foretell an era of gospel universality and of freedom from the tyranny of Satan and sin. In this peaceful period the meek will inherit the earth. The meek, remnant survivors whom God's angels had sealed during the first tribulation will live chaste lives and beget children on a transformed and purified earth. The influence of sin will be modified and God's name will be honored. Diseases and maladies of various sorts will completely disappear, and the "lame will leap like the stag," justice and peace shall kiss, and the land shall produce abundant fruit, for God has blessed his people.

---

[136] Emmerich, Vol. I, pp. 569, 570.

[137] La Salette, 1846.

During the Era of Peace Christ will not return to definitively reign on earth in the flesh, but will "appear" to many. As in the Book of Acts and in the Gospel of Matthew Christ made "apparitions" to his elect of the newborn Church shortly after his resurrection from the dead,[138] so during the Era so Peace Christ will appear to the remnant survivors and their offspring. Jesus will appear to many in his risen body and in the Eucharist, and his presence will especially be felt in the soul of the human creature. This interior presence of God in the soul of the human creature will empower it to experience the greatest mystical gift God has given the world, the gift of Living in the Divine Will. This gift is a continuous participation in the eternal operations of the three divine Persons, which has also been referred to as a "pneumatic coming," or a "new Pentecost." It is "pneumatic" because the Spirit of Jesus enters the spirit of the human creature in a new, continuous and eternal way. (For more information on the gift of Living in the Divine Will, I refer you to my latest ecclesiastically approved book, *The Splendor of Creation*, St. Andrew's Productions [2004], chapter 3.5 *ff.* To order call: 1-412-787-9735. This book is also available in Italian and Spanish, and is presently being translated into Ukrainian).

5.3   Personages in the Era of Peace

5.3.1   Great Monarch

During the era of worldwide peace, the laws and the common good will be secured under a new monarch and under a newly elected pontiff. The monarch, or king, shall be of French descent, but not French in the narrow sense, for prophecies suggest that he will come from Belgium and will be of Austrian and German blood as well. He will establish a theocracy in which the Church and state are united under the one God. The monarch will champion the newly elected pope's mission of re-evangelizing those who, by God's election, have survived the war and the comet.

---

[138] Acts 1:3, Mt. 27:51-53.

The 15th century Italian mystic St. Francis of Paola affirms:

> By the grace of the Almighty, the Great Monarch
> will annihilate heretics and unbelievers. He will
> have a great army, and angels will fight at his
> side. He will be like the sun among the stars. His
> influence will spread over the whole earth. All
> in all, there will be on earth twelve Kings, one
> Emporer, one Pope and a few princes. They will
> all lead holy lives.[139]

The 17th century mystic Venerable Bartholomew Holzhauser affirms:

> The fifth period of the Church, which began circa
> 1520, will end with the arrival of the Holy Pope
> and of the powerful monarch who is called 'Help
> from God' because he will restore everything
> [in Christ]... The sixth period of the Church
> will begin with the powerful monarch and the
> holy Pontiff... and it will last until the revelation
> of [the final] Antichrist. In this period God
> will console his Holy Church for the affliction
> of the great tribulation which she has endured
> during the fifth period. All nations will become
> Catholic. Vocations will be abundant as never
> before, and all men will seek only the Kingdom
> of God and his justice.[140]

> There will arise a valiant King anointed by God.
> He will be a Catholic and a descendant of Louis
> IX, yet a descendant also of an imperial German
> family, born in exile. He will rule supreme in
> temporal matters. The Pope will rule in spiritual
> matters at the same time... All nations will
> adore the Lord according to Catholic teaching...

[139] Yves, p.38.

[140] Yves, p.38-40, cf. also Venerable Bartholomew Holzhauser, 17th century.
Apocalypsin, Ven. Bartholomew Holzhauser, 1850, p.69.

> People will love justice, and peace will reign over
> the whole earth, for Divine Power will bind
> Satan for many years.[141]

The 19th century mystic St. Bertina Bequillon writes:

> A saint raises his arms to heaven; he allays the
> wrath of God. He ascends the throne of Peter.
> At the same time, the great monarch ascends the
> throne of his ancestors. All is quiet now. Altars
> are set up again; religion comes to life again.
> What I see now is so wonderful that I am unable
> to express it"[142]

Melanie Calvat of La Salette remarks:

> After a frightful war a Great King will arise and
> his reign will be marked by a wonderful peace
> and a great religious revival.[143]

5.3.2   Last Pontiffs

The new pope of the Era of Peace will reform the clergy. Blessed
Emmerich foresaw the new pope's election and efforts of dispelling the
smoke of Satan that had entered the Church:

> When the combat on earth was over... I saw a
> new pope, earnest and energetic. I saw... a great
> many bad bishops and pastors expelled by him...
> I saw the petition: "Lord, Thy Kingdom come,"
> being verified (emphasis added).[144]

---

[141] Ibid., p.44.

[142] (St. Bertina Bequillon). *Voix Prophetiques*, Curicquo, 1872, Vol. 1, p. 472.

[143] Ibid., p. 13.

[144] Emmerich, Vol. I, pp. 569, 570.

The newly elected pope will be firm and will restore the former disciplines and Traditions that Antichrist mocked. He will censure bad bishops, pastors and laypersons who refuse to submit to God's rule. Earlier I gave evidence to support the election of a new pontiff in the Era of Peace. Such an assertion is predicated on the prophecy of St. Malachy. St. Malachy O'Morgair was the Archbishop of Armagh, Ireland, who died in 1148. Malachy was a good friend of St. Bernard of Clairvaux and when he had visited Pope Innocent II in Rome in 1139 he was granted a vision of all the Holy Fathers of all centuries to the end of the world. He wrote down a description of each in Latin and gave the list to Pope Innocent. Nothing more is heard of the list until 1590 when a Benedictine monk, Arnold de Wyon, discovered it in the Vatican archives. Although some question its unmodified authenticity, others regard it as a reliable document. Of the 112 Popes described in the prophecy 74 had already reigned when the list was discovered. The last six popes who are given titles are listed as follows:

Pastor et Nauta ("Shepherd and Sailor"): John XXIII was chiefly concerned with the pastoral problems of his day and for this reason convened the Vatican II Council. He had come from Venice, a sailor's city, and set the Church on a new course.

Flos Florum ("Flower of Flowers"): Paul VI had a lily as his coat of arms. His arguably greatest contribution to the Church was his encyclical in defense of human life, *Humanae Vitae*. The marvelous doctrines contained in this encyclical reveal the intrinsical and grave evils of the artificial means of birth control that impede the *flowering* of life. It is no surprise that this pope who defended life, is referred to as *flos florum*.

De Mediatate Lunae ("From the Midst of the Moon" or "From the Half of the Moon"): In Scripture the moon represents a worldly kingdom, which may suggest that he was elected at a time when Satan, the prince of this world, has influence even within the church through a secret government. It has been reported that Pope John Paul I held a list of the ecclesiastical freemasons whom he wished to expel from the church, but he did not live long enough to do so. The significance of the 'half' moon may also imply his unusually brief papacy.

De Laboris Solis ("Of the Labor of the Sun"): This represents the symbol of the Book of Revelation 12:1-5, of a woman clothed with the sun, who does battle with the dragon and is in labor to give birth to a son. Pope John Paul II chose the Monfortian expression *Totus Tuus* for his coat of arms to proclaim his indefatigable devotion to Mary, who is the prophet of the End Times that does battle with the dragon. It is also indisputable that this pontiff is the third longest reigning Pope that has *labored* with marvellous intensity alongside Mary to unite Christians and to herald the Era of Peace. In his encyclical he foretells a "millennium of unifications" in which we are called to "live in the will of God."

De Gloria Olivae ("From the Glory of the Olive Tree"): This title well represents the glorious period of peace and unity represented by the olive. It effectively suggests that the rule of Pope Benedict XVI will introduce us to the Era of Peace. Despite the advanced age of the recent papal elect, in choosing the name Benedict XVI, Cardinal Joseph Ratzinger linked his pontificate to two great evangelizers. On April 19, 2005 Bishop Cipriano Calderon, retired vicepresident of the Pontifical Commission for Latin America, said in statements: "The novelty of this Pontiff lies already in the name chosen: He succeeds Benedict XV, who chose this name in honor of St. Benedict, patron of Europe and great evangelizer of his time. If Benedict evangelized the first Medieval Age, Benedict XV evangelized the modern age, and now *Benedict XVI will be the evangelizer of the new millennium.*" It is noteworthy that Pope Benedict XV, *Giacomo della Chiesa*, appealed for peace, reformed the clergy and established the octave of prayer *for Christian unity* in 1916.

Petrus Romanus ("Peter the Roman"): The last Pope bears the name that reflects the office of the very first pope, and for that matter, an office marked by the last persecutions of Antichrist (Gog and Magog that arise after the Era of Peace), and the last judgment. The prophecy concludes: "In the final persecution of the Holy Roman Church there shall reign Peter the Roman who will feed his flock amid many tribulations, after which the seven-hilled city will be destroyed and the terrible judge will judge the people."

Indeed some may question the credibility of Malachi's vision, as perhaps only one pope reigning for a period of peace symbolized by a thousand years would seem improbable. To this question I submit two possibilities: one, that the thousand years' peace is not a literal representation of time, but an allegorical rendering to indicate a long duration of peace with God and creation (for a proper understanding of the thousand years, and for a complete listing of its characteristics I refer you to Chapter 4 of the aforementioned book, *The Splendor of Creation*);[145] two, that St. Malachi's list of future pontiffs ends not with the end of the world, but with the beginning of the Era of Peace. Furthermore, if Malachi's documented vision of all popes is indeed unmodified, Sacred Scripture and the writings of the early Church Fathers suggest a qualitative and quantitative melioration of the lives of those that enter into and experience the Era of Peace.[146]

---

[145]   *The Splendor of Creation*, Rev. J. Iannuzzi, St. Andrew's Productions, McKees Rocks, PA 15136, tel. (412) 787-9735. This book is also available in Italian and Spanish, and is presently being translated into Ukrainian.

[146]   "There shall no more be an infant of days there, nor an old man that shall not fill up his days; for the child shall die a hundred years old... For as the days of the tree of life, so shall be the days of My people, and the works of their hands shall be multiplied. My elect shall not labor in vain, nor bring forth children for a curse; for they shall be a righteous seed blessed by the Lord, and their posterity with them" (St. Justin Martyr, "Dialogue with Trypho," The Fathers of the Church [Christian Heritage, 1948] pp. 277-278); "Also there shall not be any immature one, nor an old man who does not fulfill his time; for the youth shall be of a hundred years old..." (St. Irenaeus of Lyons, "Adversus Haereses," Bk. 34, Ch. 4; The Fathers of the Church [NY: CIMA Publishing Co., 1947]); "As the years of a tree, so the years of my people... They shall not toil in vain nor beget children for sudden destruction; for a race blessed by the Lord are they and their offspring" (Is 54:1; cf. also Is 65:22-23).

CHAPTER 6

Antichrist in the New Testament

6.1 The Gospel of Matthew

After exposing the antichristian tribulation before the Era of Peace, the Gospel of Matthew recalls the thousand years' peace of Revelation 20. Matthew lists three questions posed to Jesus by his disciples that reveal the chronology of events leading up to the final tribulation and triumph and the end of the age. These questions determine the time of the temple's destruction, the sign of Christ's coming and finally the end of the age:

> Tell us, when will this happen, and what sign will there be of your coming, and of the end of the age?[147]

The responses to these questions are presented in verse sequence: When will all this happen (when will the destruction of the temple occur)? What sign will there be of his coming? What sign will there be of the end of the age?

> **What sign will there be of the end of the age? Mt. 24:6-14:** "You will hear of wars and reports of wars; see that you are not alarmed, for these things must happen, but it will not yet be the end. Nation will rise against nation, and

---

[147] Mt 24:3.

> kingdom against kingdom; there will be famines
> and earthquakes from place to place. All these
> things are the beginning of the labor pains. Then
> they will hand you over to persecution, and they
> will kill you. You will be hated by all nations
> because of My name. And then many will be led
> into sin; they will betray and hate one another.
> Many false prophets will arise and deceive many,
> and because of the increase of evildoing, the
> love of many will grow cold. But the one who
> perseveres to the end will be saved. *And this
> gospel of the kingdom will be preached throughout
> the world as a witness to all nations, and then the
> end will come."*

In the first verses of Matthew's 24th chapter, Jesus refers to the universal preaching of the Gospel and its preceding tribulation, thus recalling many Scriptural references to an Era of Peace when Christ will be known and loved in all the earth:

> So shall your rule be known *upon the earth*, your
> saving power among *all the nations*.[148]

> I will make you a light to *the nations* that my
> salvation may reach to *the ends of the earth*.[149]

> See, the Lord proclaims to *the ends of the earth*:
> Say to daughter Zion, 'Your savior comes!'[150]

Recent terrorism demonstrates that the proclamation of the gospel has not been so effectively preached[151] to all nations[152] that God's power

---

[148] Ps 67:3.

[149] Is 49:6.

[150] Is 62:11.

[151] Mt 24:14.

[152] Mk 13:10.

and glory are known to the ends of the earth. Such an accomplishment, the Church teaches, will be fully achieved by the glorified Spirit of Christ who, through a new Pentecost, establishes the reign of God's will in man.[153] Jesus alludes to this when placing the earth's consummation after the universal preaching of the gospel: *"This gospel of the kingdom will be preached throughout the world as a witness to all nations, and then the end will come."*

> **When will all this happen; when will the destruction of the temple occur? Mt. 24:15-27:**
> *"When you see the desolating abomination spoken of through Daniel the prophet standing in the holy place* (let the reader understand), then those in Judea must flee to the mountains, a person on the housetop must not go down to get things out of his house, a person in the field must not return to get his cloak. Woe to the pregnant women and nursing mothers in those days. Pray that your flight not be in winter or on the Sabbath, for at that time there will be great tribulation, *such as has not been since the beginning of the world until now, nor ever will be.* And if those days had not been shortened, no one would be saved; but for the sake for the elect they will be shortened… For *just as lightning comes from the east and is seen as far as the west, so will the coming of the Son of Man be.* Wherever the corpse is, there the vultures will gather."

Not only does Matthew provide glimpses of the events preceding the era of global evangelization; he also unmasks Satan's last individual incarnation in Daniel's "desolating abomination." Having deceived the inhabitants of the earth with the signs he performs, the last Antichrist will raise the pagan nations to pillage and plunder the house of Israel. This period, Jesus recalls, will be filled with great tribulation *"such as has not been since the beginning of the world until now, nor ever will be."* For the

---

[153] *The Teaching of the Catholic Church: A Summary of Catholic Doctrine,* Ibid.

evil one is especially filled with purely satanic hatred at the sight of all mankind worshipping Christ toward the end of the Era of Peace. Having been released from confinement, Satan, with utmost spite, will draw his agents of seduction to ruin God's work for the last time. On the heels of the greatest tribulation, shortened for the sake of the elect, Jesus will return from heaven in glory to inaugurate the new and eternal Jerusalem in a way that Matthew describes as sudden as lightning, which "comes from the east and is seen as far as the west."

Matthew's knowledge of the Book of Daniel is self-evident. The New American Bible reads, "The desolating abomination (of Mt. 24) ... is referred to in Dn. 12,11 LXX as the 'desolating abomination' and the same Greek term is used here."[154] In view of the prophecies of Mt. 24 and Daniel 12:11, one may estimate the probable time of Antichrist's final reign: "From the time that the daily sacrifice is abolished and the horrible abomination is set up, there shall be one thousand two hundred and ninety days." In essence, of the three and a half years a short time will be laid aside in the end for the faithful remnant to gather together in prayer for the final battle in which St. Michael with his angels will defeat Satan and his demons (Dn. 12:1). Under the biblical name of *Gog*, the last and most furious Antichrist will resume a world-wide persecution against God and his holy place, after the manner of his predecessor, the False Prophet who, before the Era of Peace, laid the foundations for his final coming.

> **What sign will there be of his coming? Mt. 24:29-31:** "Immediately after the tribulation of those days, the sun will be darkened, and the moon will not give its light, and the stars will fall from the sky, and the powers of the heavens will be shaken. And then the sign of the Son of Man will appear in heaven, and all the tribes of the earth will mourn, and they will see the Son of Man coming upon the clouds of heaven with power and great glory. And he will send out his angels with a trumpet blast, and they will gather

---

[154] *The New American Bible*, Ibid., cf. footnote of Mt 24:15.

his elect from the four winds, from one end of
the heavens to the other."

The days of darkness[155] preceding Satan's last manifestation in
Gog and Magog will be occasioned by the darkening of the sun, the moon
and the stars. After Satan is definitively defeated and Gog and Magog
consumed by fire, they are then cast into the pool of fire together with the
False Prophet and the Beast.[156] Only then will God's eternal victory be
celebrated in the New Heavens and New Earth, where no temple is found
save the temple of the Lamb, who gives light and life to the temples of our
bodies. These temples of the Holy Spirit will radiate light everywhere,
like living tabernacles imbued with the fullness of Christ's divinity:

> Then I saw a new heaven and a new earth... I also
> saw the holy city, a new Jerusalem, coming down
> out of heaven from God...I saw no temple in the
> city, for its temple is the Lord God almighty and
> the Lamb.[157]

> The city had no need of sun or moon to shine
> on it, for the glory of God gave it light...nor will
> they need light from lamp or sun, for the Lord
> God shall give them light and they shall reign
> forever and ever.[158]

If several early Church Fathers, Doctors and Writers considered
Satan's two-fold individual incarnation in the False Prophet and Gog, it
was to forewarn their disciples of the ordeals they would endure. Their
writings breathe the spirit of the martyrs, full of hope for a world shorn of
sin. They remind all that as a tempest serves to purify air and fire serves
to purify soil, so God uses the calamities and chastisements brought on by
sin to transform and renew the present earth.

---

[155]   Acts 2: 17-21; Jl 2:1-3.

[156]   Rev 20:9-10.

[157]   Rev 21:1-2, 22.

[158]   Rev 21:23; 22:5.

6.2   The Pauline Epistles

> We ask you, brothers, with regard to the coming
> of our Lord Jesus Christ and our assembling
> with him, not to be shaken out of your minds
> suddenly... that the day of the Lord is at hand.
> Let no one deceive you in any way. *For unless the*
> *apostasy comes first and the lawless one is revealed,*
> *the one doomed to perdition... whom the Lord*
> *[Jesus] will kill with the breath of his mouth and*
> *render powerless by the manifestation of his coming...*
> that all who have not believed the truth but have
> approved wrongdoing may be condemned... God
> chose you as the first fruits...[159]

As indicated earlier, Paul's reference to "the apostasy," "the lawless
one" and "one doomed to perdition," much like Matthew and Mark, points
to the Book of Daniel. It is worthy of mention that Daniel's "abomination
of desolation" appears at the end of the world, that is, *after* the Era of Peace.
It is related in Mathew's Gospel as the greatest tribulation the world will
ever experience, and in Daniel as "a time of unsurpassed distress," when
God's holy temple is desecrated—the temple God's remnant constructed
during the era,[160] and after which "all these things should end." Paul's
illustration of the aftermath of Satan's final unleashing of evil suddenly
turns in favor of God's elect:

> For we believe that Jesus died and rose, so too
> will God, through Jesus, bring with him those
> who have fallen asleep. Indeed, we tell you this,
> on the word of the Lord, that *we who are alive,*
> *who are left until the coming of the Lord,* will surely
> not precede those who have fallen asleep. For the
> Lord himself, with a word of command, with the
> voice of an Archangel and with the trumpet of
> God, will come down from heaven, and the dead

---

[159] 2 Thes 2:1-13.

[160] Ez 40ff; Dn 12:11-13.

in Christ will rise first. Then we who are alive, who are left, will be caught up together with them in the clouds to meet the Lord in the clouds. Thus we shall always be with the Lord.[161]

In this passage, the trumpet of God that ushers in our Lord's return alludes to the Book of Revelation, among whose many trumpets only one ushers in the Final Judgment:

The seventh angel blew his trumpet. There were loud voices in heaven, saying, 'The kingdom of the world now belongs to our Lord and to his Anointed, and he will reign forever and ever.' The twenty-four elders who sat on their thrones before God...said: 'We give thanks to you, Lord God almighty... For you... have established your reign... Your wrath has come, and the time to judge the dead.'[162]

Both the Pauline and Johannine trumpet exhibit striking similarities. They not only indicate the Lord's final return in glory, but also announce his Final Judgment on the living and the dead. Unlike the Particular Judgment before the Era of Peace, the final trumpet signals the Final Judgment and the beginning of Christ's eternal reign with the human race in the new and eternal Jerusalem.

6.3   The Letter of Peter

The first Letter of Peter confirms Satan's progressive and final defeat in synoptic fashion through a chronology of the three heavens and three earths. Mary's role in the salvation of souls during earth's final hours completes her birth pangs, and reveals her Son's triumphant return in glory in the New Heavens and New Earth. The demarcations in brackets separate these three Petrine stages:

---

[161] 1 Thes 4:14-18.

[162] Rev 11:15-19.

The heavens existed of old and earth was formed out of water *[1st heavens & earth]...* the world that then existed was destroyed, deluged with water *[end of 1st heavens & earth: the Particular Judgment of the nonbelievers, and the remnant of Noah's family].* The present heavens and earth *[2nd heavens and earth]*[163] have been reserved by the same word for fire, kept for the day of destruction of the godless... one day is like a thousand years and a thousand years like one day... *[end of 2nd heavens & earth: the Particular Judgment of nonbelievers, and the remnant of the era of peace].* But the Day of the Lord will come like a thief, and then the heavens will pass away with a mighty roar and the elements will be dissolved by fire, and the earth and everything done on it will be found out... But according to his promise we await new heavens and a new earth" *[3rd heavens & earth: the Parousia, the General Judgment of all the living and the dead, and the remnant of the New Jerusalem, the New Heavens and New Earth].*[164]

---

[163]   St. Peter's 2nd heavens & earth represents the period of the institutional Church that extends from the time of Christ to the end of time. Since the era of peace occurs within time, it represents the period of the Church when the sacraments are revered by all the earth's inhabitants, when the 2nd heavens and 2nd earth approach their zenith, and when creation will be set free from its slavery to corruption and enjoy the glorious freedom of the sons of God.

[164]   2 Pt 3:5-13.

CHAPTER 7

ANTICHRIST AFTER THE
ERA OF PEACE

7.1   Etymology

In Revelation 20:7 St. John refers to the last Antichrist as "Gog." It is interesting to note that the name "Gog" is not a name that appears only in the Book of Revelation. We first encounter references to Gog in the Old Testament. It is here that the first vestiges of Gog's personality, purpose and place of origin are revealed. In the Book of Numbers 22:6, Balak, the avaricious King of Moab, asks the prophet Balaam to curse Israel. Despite Balak's request, Balaam blesses Israel three times and prophesies, *"the King of Israel shall be higher than Agag"* (an antichrist and precursor of Gog), *and his kingdom shall be exalted."*[165] In 1 Sam. 15:7-8 we read of Agag's fate: *"Saul routed Amalek… He took Agag, king of Amalek… He cut Agag down before the Lord in Gilgal."* In chapters 3 and 4 of the Book of Deuteronomy, we encounter another precursor of Gog who goes by the name of *"Og"* (Γὼγ), the wealthy King of Bashan. Og shares the same fate as Agag in that he too is defeated and his land is confiscated and given over to the Israelites whom he had oppressed. In the Book of Esther 3 Agag's name resurfaces in the person of Haman the *"Agagite,"* to whom Mordecai refuses honor and who is killed by hanging through the intervention of Esther. Interestingly, the Hebrews regarded Haman the *Agagite* as a descendent of King *Agag*. In the Books of Ezekiel 38-39

---

[165] Septuagint Bible, *Septuaginta*, 1d est Vetus Testamentum graece iuxta LXX interpretes; edidit Alfred Rahls; Duo volumina in uno; Deutsche Bibelgesellschaft, Stuttgart, Germany, 1979. Nm 24:1-7. 169 Otto, Helen. *When Heaven Broke the Seals and Opened the Scrolls*, Verenikia Press, Rockhill, SC 1998, inter alia.

and Revelation 20:8 reference is made to "Gog" (Γώγ) who, much like his antichrist predecessors, usurps power, oppresses Israel, and confiscates booty and land, only to be stripped of it when he is defeated.

Now all of these references to the Old Testament antichrists that are descriptively related culminate in the person of *Gog* in the Book of Revelation. Biblical etymology demonstrates that the characteristics possessed by *Agag, Og* and Hamaan the *Agagite* hold the key that unlocks the mystery of the person of *Gog* in the Book of Revelation. In the Hebrew tongue *Agag, Og* and *Gog* not only possess the same individual traits, but they include Gog's nature, purpose and place of origin. In Dt 3:1.13; 4:47 of the Septuagint version (Greek Bible), Gog stands for the Hebrew Og (Γώγ: the king of Bashan). In both the Old and New Testaments the traits of *Agag, Og* and *Gog* coalesce as each represents an atheistic male tyrant whose fame is founded on deception and the usurpation of power, who despises Israel (God's Church on earth), and who enjoys excessive material wealth.

In the Septuagint version the *Gog* of Ezekiel and Revelation[166] is a satanic individual who, in the end times, leads the evil nations, known as *Magog*, in battle against God and his holy ones. *Magog* first appears in Genesis 10:2, where it is listed as the name of the offspring of Noah's son Japheth. Linguistically, the Japhethites were a race that developed in a settlement after Japheth's offspring named Magog, located in the regions of modern India, Iran and Europe.[167] However, Magog, as a race and nation, has since disappeared from history. In their work of retracing Magog's lineage, scholars have concluded that it is as much a reality today as it was in the days of Japheth. Old-New Testament links reveal the place from which Gog arises – the lands "east of the Jordon: from Aroer on the edge of the Wadi Arnon to Mount Sion and all the Arabah east of the Jordan, as far as the Arabah Sea under the slopes of Pisgah."[168]

---

[166] Although Ezekiel's Gog bears overwhelming similarities to the Gog of Revelation, Ezekiel's chapter sequence places Gog before the construction of the temple, and Revelation follows the temple's profanation and destruction with his reappearance.

[167] When Heaven Broke the Seals, Ibid.

[168] Duet 4:47-49. Several Church Fathers and the La Salette message affirm that the

Thanks to the inspired biblical authors who kept track of the spiritual line of descent of the Gogs of the Old Testament, we are able to disclose the characteristics of "the spirit of antichrist" in its incarnations as portrayed in the Books of Daniel, Ezekiel, Matthew, Mark, Revelation and the 2nd Letter to the Thessalonians. A careful study of Sacred Scripture reveals the Johannine "spirit of antichrist" is a concept that finds its individual embodiment in the *Gogs* of the Old Testament Books of Nm 24; Dt 3:4; 1 Sam 15ff, Est 3ff; and Ez 38, and again in the New Testament Book of Rev 19:11.15.20-21; 20:4-5.7-8. Though the Old Testament personages *Agag, Og* and Haman the *Agagite* are dead, their satanic *spirit* re-emerges in the persons of the *False Prophet* and *Gog* of the Book of Revelation.

When posited in their biblio-historical settings, the *False Prophet* and *Gog* emerge as the biblical equivalent of two end-time Antichrists, respectively arising from the *Beast* and the land of *Magog*. The Church's early Tradition identifies the *False Prophet* and *Gog* as individual Antichrists, and the *Beast* and *Magog* as Antichrist's collective spirit or host of evil nations that ensure his rise to global power. The *Beast* represents the evil nations in cahoots with the *False Prophet* that are cast into the fiery pool burning with sulfur before the Era of Peace,[169] while *Magog*, on the other hand, represents the evil nations in consort with *Gog* that are thrown into the fiery pool after the Era of Peace.[170] As indicated earlier, the Church's early Tradition identifies the False Prophet and Gog as individual Antichrists, and the Beast and Magog as their collective spirit or host of evil nations that ensure their rise to global power.

St. Vincent Ferrer states that the False Prophet is the precursor of the fiercest Antichrist (Gog) that follows him:

> When *the false prophet, the precursor of Antichrist*
> comes, all who are not confirmed will apostatize,

Antichrist will be of Hebrew descent.

[169] Rev. 19:20.

[170] Rev. 20:9-10.

while those who are confirmed will stand fast
in their faith, and only a few will renounce
Christ.[171]

St. Irenaeus of Lyons affirms that the last and fiercest Antichrist
will be endowed with all the power of the devil:

> For he (Antichrist) *being endued with all the*
> *power of the devil*, shall come, not as a righteous
> king… but an impious, unjust, and lawless one;
> as an apostate, iniquitous and murderous; as a
> robber, *concentrating in himself all satanic apostasy*,
> and setting aside idols to persuade men that he
> himself is God, raising up himself a the only
> idol…"[172]

St. Thomas Aquinas (1225-1274 A.D.) reinforces Irenaeus' presentation
of the last Antichrist:

> The devil by suggestion infuses his wickedness
> *more copiously into him than into all others.*[173]

---

[171] Vincent Ferrer, *The Prophets & Our Times*, p. 155, in *Catholic Prophecy*, Tan Books
and Pub., Inc., Rockford, IL 1973, Ibid., p.30.

[172] St. Irenaeus of Lyons, "Adversus Haereses," V.33.3.4., *The Fathers of the Church*
(NY: CIMA Publishing Co., 1947), Book V, Ch.25, 1- 3. In his works Irenaeus
often blends the characteristics and personages of the periods before and after the
era of peace. This blending leaves the reader with the impression that there is but
one Antichrist figure, whereas St. John, early Tradition and, more recently, Cardinal
Ratzinger suggest that there is more than one Antichrist figure. On the one hand,
Irenaeus affirms that Antichrist arises before the era of peace, or "the seventh day true
Sabbath rest," thereby suggesting the False Prophet (*Adversus Haereses*, The Fathers
of the Church, Ibid., Bk. 28, Ch. 3; Bk. 30,4; Bk. 33,2.). On the other hand, Irenaeus
affirms that Antichrist will be endued with *all* the power of the devil (Ibid., Book V,
Ch.25, 1-3), thereby suggesting Satan's last and fiercest incarnation in Gog.

[173] *Summa Theologica*, Thomas Aquinas, Part III, Q. 8, Art. 8, Benzinger Bros. New
York 1947, Vol. II, p.2081.

Admittedly, the Church Fathers and early Ecclesiastical Writers do not adopt the biblical binomial Gog-Magog, yet it is suggested in their writings, as they offer a two-fold incarnation of the spirit of Satan. The writings of St. John the Apostle and Lactantius separate Antichrist's final two incarnations with an intermediary Era of Peace, and Lactantius uses a pair of judgments, which he calls the Lord's "great judgment" and "last judgment," to distinguish them. St. John reveals in the Book of Revelation:

> *The beast* was caught and with it *the false prophet*... The two were thrown alive into the fiery pool burning with sulfur. The rest were killed by the sword that came out of the mouth of the one riding on the horse... I also saw some of the souls who were beheaded… they came to life and they reigned with Christ for *a thousand years*… When the thousand years are completed, Satan will be released from his prison. He will go out to deceive the nations at the four corners of the earth, *Gog and Magog*, to gather them for battle.[174]

The earliest Church Father and the first successor to St. Peter as pope is St. Clement of Rome who writes of the Antichrist before *and* after the Era of Peace:

> A *false prophet* must first come from some deceiver; and then, in like manner, after the removal of the holy place, the true Gospel must be secretly sent abroad for the rectification of the heresies that shall be. *After this*, also, towards the end, *Antichrist* must first come, and then our Jesus must be revealed to be indeed the Christ; and after this, the eternal light having sprung up, all the things of darkness must disappear.[175]

---

[174] Rev 19:11.15.20-21; 20:4-5.7-8.

[175] St. Clement of Rome, in The Early Church Fathers and Other Works, Ibid., The Clementine Homilies, Homily II, *First the Worse, Then the Better*, Ch. XVII.

The 4th century Ecclesiastical Writer Lactantius also writes of the Antichrist before and after the thousand years of peace:

> Therefore, the Son of the most high and mighty God… shall have destroyed unrighteousness, and executed His great judgment, and shall have recalled to life the righteous, who… will be engaged among men a thousand years, and will rule them with most just command… Also *the prince of devils,* who is the contriver of all evils, shall be bound with chains, and shall be imprisoned during the thousand years of the heavenly rule…

> Before the end of the thousand years *the devil shall be loosed afresh* and shall assemble all the pagan nations to make war against the holy city… "Then the last anger of God shall come upon the nations, and shall utterly destroy them" and the world shall go down in a great conflagration.[176]

Earlier I traced the first appearance of Antichrist to its roots in the Church's biblio-historic accounts, and in the works of Ss. John and Hippolytus who refer to him as the False Prophet. I also traced Gog's lineage from the Old Testament books, where one soon discovers that the False Prophet's royal power, wealth and hatred toward the house of Israel are inherited from Agag, Og and Gog of the Old Testament. This ancestral succession of the "spirit of Satan" from one evil individual to another throughout the Old and New Testaments, gives Cardinal Ratzinger (Pope Benedict XVI) reason to affirm that Antichrist "cannot be restricted to any single individual. One and the same he wears many masks in each generation."[177] In fact, Scripture and Tradition indicate that an Antichrist will appear *after* the Era of Peace who will exceed his False Prophet predecessor by his usurpation of power, material wealth and

---

[176] Lactantius, "The Divine Institutes", *The Ante-Nicene Fathers* (Peabody, MA: Henrickson Pub., 1995), Vol. 7, p. 211.

[177] Johann Auer, and Joseph Ratzinger, Dogmatic Theology, Eschatology 9 (Catholic University of America Press, 1988), pp.199-200.

hatred toward God's church on earth. And biblical parallels poignantly demonstrate that with each historic manifestation of Antichrist there is an intensification of evil, for the world's hostility to Christ will not diminish but will increase dramatically. Thus the final appearance of Antichrist will be a time of tribulation like no other the world has known.

St. John the Apostle, Tertullian and Lactantius place Antichrist's final appearance *after* the gospel is proclaimed to the ends of the earth and shortly *before* the earth's consummation. Additionally, the writings of the eminent Church Doctors St. John Damascene, St. Robert Bellarmine and St. Bridget of Sweden (1303-1373) re-echo the last manifestation of Satan *at the end of the era*, and shortly before the resurrection of the dead and the Final Judgment:[178]

The prophet Ezekiel reveals:

> *The gospel, then, must first be preached to all nations, and then that wicked one shall be revealed:* whose coming is according to the working of Satan.[179]

St. Biridget of Sweden remarks:

> Before Antichrist comes, the portals of faith will be open to great numbers of pagans.[180]

St. Robert Bellarmine affirms:

> For Antichrist shall come a short time before the end of the world... *after Antichrist at once comes the last judgment.*[181]

---

[178] Ez 38-39; Rev 20.

[179] *De Fide Orthodoxa*, St. John Damascene, in "The Fathers of the Church, Vol. 37 (Pub: The Fathers of the Church, Inc. N.Y. Trans. By Federick H. Chase, Jr. 1958) p. 399.

[180] *Life and Revelations of St. Bridget*, Klarus, Regensburg, Mainx, 1833, VIII, p.168.

[181] St. Robert Bellarmine, *Opera Omnia, Disputationum Roberti Bellarmini, De Controversiis* [3 vol.] Chrisitianae Fidei Tomus Primus, Liner Tertius, De Summo

Here we are not simply dealing with another incarnation of the spirit of Satan, but with the greatest incarnation of Satan in the person of Gog. Sacred Scripture and the writings of early Tradition make it abundantly clear that Antichrist after the Era of Peace exceeds his predecessors in cunning, wealth, power and evil. When Satan is released from confinement toward the end of the Era of Peace, and after the offspring of the remnant survivors have repopulated the earth, Gog will gather the evil nations, known as Magog, to crush the holy offspring of the remnant survivors.[182] It will be Satan's last, pathetic attempt to destroy Christ's plans of receiving his Church in her immaculate state. The book of Revelation reveals:

> When the thousand years are completed, Satan will be released from his prison. He will go out to deceive the nations at the four corners of the earth, Gog and Magog, to gather them for battle; their number is like the sands of the sea.[183]

As quoted earlier, St. Clement of Rome affirms, "A *false prophet* must first come... *After this,* also... *Antichrist* must... come, and then our Jesus must be revealed."[184] St. Augustine also writes of Antichrist's last reprisal after the thousand years of peace:

> We shall indeed be able to interpret the words, "The priests of God and of Christ shall reign with Him a thousand years; and *when the thousand years shall be finished, Satan shall be loosed out of his prison;*" for thus they signify that the reign of the saints and the bondage of the devil shall cease simultaneously... And therefore

---

Pontifice, 1856, caput VI, in *Trial, Tribulation & Triumph, Before, During and after Antichrist*, Desmond Birch, Queenship Publishing, 1996, p.515.

[182] Ez 38-39; Rv. 20.

[183] Rev 20:1-9.

[184] St. Clement of Rome, in The Early Church Fathers and Other Works, Ibid., The Clementine Homilies, Homily II, *First the Worse, Then the Better*, Ch. XVII.

during these three years and a half the souls of
those who were slain for His testimony, both
those which formerly passed from the body and
those which shall pass in that *last persecution*,
shall reign with Him till the mortal world come
to an end, and pass into that kingdom in which
there shall be no death.

As therefore there went out from the Church
many heretics, whom John calls "many
antichrists," at that time prior to the end, and
which John calls "the last time," so in the end
they shall go out who do not belong to Christ,
but to that *last Antichrist*, and then he shall be
revealed... *For then shall Satan be loosed, and
by means of that Antichrist* shall work with all
power in a lying though a wonderful manner...
They shall be judged in that last and manifest
judgment administered by Jesus Christ, who was
Himself most unjustly judged and shall most
justly judge.[185]

As Jesus comes twice in the flesh to publicly commence and
conclude the sacramental economy of salvation for the human race, so
Satan comes twice to ape Jesus' Incarnation on a global scale through his
own incarnation in the False Prophet of Revelation 19, and to impede
Jesus' return in glory in the Gog of Revelation 20.

7.2   The Final Tribulation and Triumph

Sacred Scripture and the apostolic Tradition present an
eschatological blending of two worldwide antichristian tribulations. The
first tribulation leads to the Particular Judgment of all nonbelievers, and
is followed by an Era of Peace, the final tribulation, and the General
Judgment. It is only after the Era of Peace, or God's Sabbath Rest with

---

[185] St. Augustine, *The Anti-Nicene Fathers*, Ibid., City of God, Book XX, Chs. 13, 19.

creation, that Satan is released and, with the nations at his disposal, "surrounds the camp of the holy ones and the beloved city" at the final tribulation.[186]

7.2.1   Satan loosed from Prison and the Defection from the Faith

The Book of Revelation reveals:

> When the thousand years are completed, Satan will be released from his prison. He will go out to deceive the nations at the four corners of the earth, *Gog and Magog,* to gather them for battle.[187]

As to how it is possible that God's holy and immaculate Church should suffer devastation from the "pagan nations" during the era that is filled with peace and holiness, the response hinges on two realities: Satan's release from confinement and God's irrevocable gift of free will. Ezekiel reminds us that the elect who enter into this universal Era of Peace will be of one mind and heart, led by the Spirit of God in the faithful observance of his will, ordinances and decrees.[188] So although evil remains a potential threat throughout the era, God's unique outpouring of grace will modify its influence in man and in creation until the end of the era, when Satan is released. However, such peace and holiness is not absolutely guaranteed, especially not to those that are alive at the end of the era. The Scripture scholar A. Theissen concludes that in his epistles that address the unification of the end times, Paul neither refers to the end of history nor to a salvation that no longer stands in need of God's mercy. Paul's review of the divine plan of salvation and the conversion of the Jewish nation reveals that some, numbered among the elect, will revert to a lifestyle of sin:[189]

---

[186]   Rev 20:7-9.

[187]   Rev 19:11.15.20-21; 20:4-5.7-8

[188]   Ez 36:27.

[189]   Rom 11:25.

> The time will come when the present problem
> of Israel's exclusion from the salvation of
> the Messiah will cease to exist because of
> her conversion, which will follow upon the
> conversion of the Gentiles… *"Fullness (pleroma)*
> *of the Gentiles" need not be pressed so as to mean*
> *every individual, nor all "Israel."*[190]

While the peaceful remnant that inherits God's land in the Era of Peace will be "a holy nation," some of its offspring will be less holy, as they will lose the faith of their fathers. Though God holds out to all the gift of Living in the Divine Will, not all will accept this gift in the same measure, and toward the end of the era some will even reject this gift. Since the era constitutes a portion of mankind's history—in which the human creature is endowed with special graces, save the grace of impeccability that is proper to the next life—the human creature is not exempt from the influence of evil. Once Satan is released toward the end of the era, he will exercise his evil influence over man's free will with greater intensity than in preceding centuries.

A fitting analogy to explain the infiltration of pagan nations shortly before the end of the era is found in Israel's refusal to accept God's mercy. Despite God's prodigies in the Old Testament, of changing water into blood, of transforming Moses' staff into a serpent, of dividing the Red Sea and sending down manna and quail, within six weeks the Israelites were prostrate before a golden calf. If the people of God, set apart from all other nations to be peculiarly his own, could become so quickly estranged from God, what is to keep his elect from following their example? Only those who freely submit their will to God's eternal will shall have the strength from on high to resist Antichrist's final assault.

7.2.2   Gathering of Pagan Nations and the Final Battle

The complimentary biblical texts from the Books of Revelation and Ezekiel link Satan's final assault to Gog and Magog who surround

---

[190]   A. Theissen, *Catholic Commentary on Holy Scripture*, Toronto, N.Y. Edinburgh, Thomas Nelson & Sons, 1953, pp. 1072, 1073.

the peaceful and assembled "camp of the beloved."[191] The prophet Ezekiel attributes the invasion of the camp of the holy ones to a band of northern nations besieging remnant Israel in the last days:

> Thus the word of the Lord came to me: Son of man, turn toward *Gog [the land of Magog], the chief prince of Meschech and Tubal,* and prophesy against him:[192] Thus says the Lord God: See! I am coming at you, Gog, chief prince of Meshech and Tubal. I will lead you forth with all your army, horses and riders all handsomely outfitted, a great horde with bucklers and shield, all of them carrying swords... After many days you will be mustered against a nation which has survived the sword, which has been assembled from many peoples [on the mountains of Israel which were long a ruin] which has been brought forth from among the peoples and all of whom now dwell in security... a peaceful people... whose ruins were repeopled and a people gathered from the nations who dwell at the navel of the earth... and come *from your home in the recesses of the north... It is of you that I spoke in ancient times through my servants, the prophets of Israel,* who prophesied in those days that I would bring you against them. But on that day, the day when *Gog invades the land of Israel,* says the Lord God, my fury shall be aroused... before me shall tremble the fish of the sea and the birds of the air, the beasts of the field and all the reptiles that crawl on the ground, and all men who are on the land. Mountains shall be overturned, and cliffs shall tumble, and every wall shall fall to the ground.[193]

---

[191] Ez 39:1-5; Rev. 20:9.

[192] As Hippolytus uses the masculine third person singular to describe the empire of the beast, and not an individual, so Ezechiel uses the same case to describe a gathering of pagan nations known collectively as "Magog".

[193] Ez 38:1-20.

I recall the words of the 3rd century Ecclesiastical Writer Lactantius who reveals Satan's final unleashing at the end of the Era of Peace that will cause a great many to abandon the faith of their fathers:

> *Before the end of the thousand years the devil shall be loosed afresh and shall assemble all the pagan nations to make war against the holy city. He shall besiege and surround it.* "Then the last anger of God shall come upon the nations, and shall utterly destroy them"... The people of God will be concealed in the caves of the earth during the three days of destruction, until the anger of God against the nations and the last judgment shall be ended... When the thousand years shall be completed, the world shall be renewed by God, and the heavens shall be folded together, and the earth shall be changed, and God shall transform men into the similitude of angels, and they shall be white as snow; and they shall always be employed in the sight of the Almighty, and shall make offerings to their Lord, and serve Him forever. At the same time shall take place that second and public resurrection of all, in which the unrighteous shall be raised to everlasting punishments".[194]

The Church's ordinary Magisterium also describes the mystical body of Satan's black church as a collectivity of evil forces that arise in the end:[195]

---

[194] *The Divine Institutes*, Lactantius, Ante-Nicene Fathers, Henrickson Pub., Peabody, MA, 1995, Vol. 7, p. 211.

[195] "The individual antichrist of Paul... ought to be read in light of the larger picture... The Pauline argument presents a lingering dilemma to many scholars. Paul's antichrist has been considered by several modern commentators as 'a mere personification of the evil forces that will, it seems, get the upper hand at the end of the world.'" (Dom B. Orchard, *The Character of the Antichrist, A Catholic Commentary on Holy Scripture*, Catholic Hermitage Books, CN 1951 [1140-1141] – with *imprimatur* and *nihil obstat*).

Before Christ's second coming the Church must pass through the final trial that will shake the faith of many believers. The persecution that accompanies her pilgrimage on earth will unveil the 'mystery of iniquity' in the form of a religious deception offering men an apparent solution to their problems at the price of apostasy from the truth. *The supreme religious deception is that of Antichrist, a psuedomessiansim by which man glorifies himself in place of God and of his Messiah come in the flesh.*[196]

The kingdom will be fulfilled, then, not by a historic triumph of the Church through a progressive ascendancy, but *only by God's victory over the final unleashing of evil, which will cause the bride to come down from heaven.*[197]

The Last Judgment will come when Christ returns in glory. Only the Father knows the day and the hour; only he determines the moment of its coming. Then through his Son Jesus Christ he will pronounce the final word on all history ... *The Last Judgment will reveal that God's justice triumphs over all the injustices committed by his creatures and that God's love is stronger than death.*[198]

When Gog and Magog incite the final battle against Almighty God, God will cause fire to come down from heaven to consume Gog and his minions, condemning Satan, in the wretched company of Gog and Magog, the False Prophet and the Beast, to the fiery pool of burning sulfur for all eternity.[199] The judgment of God over Satan concludes the

---

[196] CCC, Ibid., 675.

[197] CCC, Ibid., 677.

[198] CCC, Ibid., 1040.

[199] Rev 20:10.

Day of the Lord and inaugurates the New Jerusalem, the New Heavens and the New Earth. Sacred Scripture reveals:

> I will work wonders in the heavens above and signs in the earth below; blood, fire and a cloud of smoke. The sun shall be turned into darkness, and the moon to blood, *before the coming of the great and splendid day of the Lord, and it shall be that everyone shall be saved who calls on the name of the Lord.*[200]

> The Day of the Lord is coming; a day of darkness and of gloom like dawn spreading over the mountains, a people numerous and mighty! ... Their like has not been from of old, nor will it be after them... before them fire devours.[201]

> With regard to the coming of the Lord Jesus Christ... (that day will not come) unless the apostasy comes first and the lawless one is revealed, the one doomed to perdition, who opposes and exalts himself above every so-called god and object of worship, so as to seat himself in the temple of God, claiming that he is a god... *whom the Lord [Jesus] will kill with the breath of his mouth and render powerless by the manifestation of his coming.*[202]

> The work of each will come to light, for the Day will disclose it. It will be revealed with fire, and the fire itself will test the quality of each one's work.[203]

---

[200] Acts 2: 17-21.

[201] Jl 2:1-3.

[202] 2 Thes 2:1-8.

[203] 1 Cor 3:13. St. Paul alludes to the Last Judgment when everyone's deeds will be brought to light.

CHAPTER 8

THE PAROUSIA AND THE FINAL JUDGMENT

In spite of a few interpolations, the historic Era of Peace and the eternal New Jerusalem emerge from the writings of the early Church Fathers, Doctors, Writers and Saints as two separate events which, though distinct, are not unrelated; indeed, the sentences of the Final Judgment cannot vary from those of the Particular Judgment.

As to where the Final Judgment will take place scholars do not know. The valley of Jehoshaphat has often been suggested in view of Joel 4:2.12 where judgment is passed from God's throne. Interestingly, the name Jehoshaphat is not geographical but symbolic, signifying the place where Yahweh judges. Just what real details lie embedded in its scriptural imagery is impossible to define. What is certain is that all men will behold God's age-old plan fulfilled and will bear witness that it is well done. The whole human race will see with their eyes and hear with their ears the justice of God's ways and the triumph of Christ who came to redeem it.

While divine revelation does not minimize the chastisements brought on by sin, it never departs from its main motif of love and mercy. What may at first appear to be an anti-Christian drama of war and bloodshed poignantly turns in favor of God's seed crushing the serpent's head. In the end all will behold God's mysterious work of converting evil to good. Without ever willing evil, God permits it for a *greater* good, as *"all things* work for good for those who love God, who are called according to his purpose."[204] The fact that God can draw good from evil is made

---

[204] Rm 8:28.

evident in the approved writings of his mystics. Jesus reveals to the Servant of God Luisa Piccarreta (1865-1947 A.D.) that original sin was permitted to bring about a *greater* good:

> Although when I created man I made him as pure and noble heavens, in the Redemption I adorned him with the brilliant stars of My wounds to cover his ugliness and make him more beautiful. I clothed him with such magnificence that his appearance *surpassed in beauty that of his original state.* This is why the Church says: "Happy fault."[205]

Jesus tells the Canadian mystic Blessed Dina Belanger (1897-1929 A.D.) that original sin will bring about a greater good:

> *The glory that my Father has received since the Redemption is, in spite of human sinfulness, far greater than if humans had never sinned,* because the reparation that I offer my Father is infinite, and it makes up infinitely for all the sins of the human race.[206]

Let us recall that God is ever ready to extend his saving hand to those who turn to him, for *"everyone shall be saved who calls on the name of the Lord."*[207] Therefore, when understood as an expression of the Good Shepherd's solemn intervention at the end of history, the Final Judgment and the Day of the Lord become a reason for rejoicing. From the preceding presentations on the False Prophet and the Beast, and Gog and Magog, a distinct pattern emerges in Satan's activity. Satan seeks to snatch at equality with God by emulating the Godhead. As the divine Word decreed from all eternity to assume an individual human nature

---

[205] Luisa Piccarreta, *Pro-manuscripts* (Milano, Italy: Assocazione del Divin Volere, 1977); February 26, 1922.

[206] Blessed Dina Bélanger, *The Autobiography*, p. 343, June 14, 1928.

[207] Acts 2: 21.

in the Incarnation of his divine Person[208] and a collective human nature in his mystical body,[209] so Satan incarnates himself in the human nature of the False Prophet and in his black church, the Beast.[210] As the divine Word decreed to reappear in his human nature at the end of history to inaugurate the immaculate Church, the New Jerusalem, so Satan reappears in the human nature of Gog to inaugurate his black church, Magog.[211] As God operates in a Trinity of divine Persons that form one divine Nature, so Satan operates in a trinity of persons that form one diabolical nature: Satan, the False Prophet and Gog.[212] As the Father's Divine Will is the essence of the three divine Persons,[213] so the three diabolic persons are animated by the diabolic will of "the dragon, the ancient serpent, which is the Devil or Satan."[214]

The question may arise as to why several early Church writers who, although aware of two individual incarnations of Satan, did not address them with equal distinction. Admittedly, some articulated two reprisals of Antichrist, before and after the Era of Peace, whereas others were less specific. Just as the Apostles, whom Jesus had promised to enlighten "in all the truth" through progressive revelations of his Spirit possessed different degrees of knowledge of God's plan of salvation, so too the Church Fathers, Doctors and Writers.

---

[208] Mt 2:23; Mk 1; Lk 1:32-33; Jn 1:14.

[209] Christ's mystical body, the Church, will achieve its state of perfection when all souls fully exercise their common priesthood thereby forming one priesthood in Christ (cf. Is 61:6; 1 Pt 2:5.9; Rev 5:10; 19:6).

[210] Rev 19:20.

[211] Rev 20:8; Ez 38-39.

[212] Rev 16:13; 20:2.10.

[213] The whole Godhead is present in whatever God does *ad extra*, or external to himself. This truth is known in theology as, *"Opera Trinitatis ad extra sunt indivisa"* (the external works of the Trinity are undivided).

[214] Rev. 20:2.

8.1 Chronology of Events

The teachings of the Church Fathers, Doctors, Writers and modern mystics reveal a chronology of events leading up to the New Jerusalem and the New Heavens and New Earth. These events extend from a Particular Judgment of non-believers, to Satan's imprisonment to the era of peace, and from Satan's final reprisal to the Final Judgment. I present these events in sequential order in tabloid form.

+ The tribulation before the Era of Peace: God destroys atheism and pronounces judgment on all nonbelievers. He casts the False Prophet and the Beast into the fiery lake and enchains Satan.
+ God spiritually recalls to life those that have died in Christ to instruct the faithful remnant that has survived the tribulation.
+ Christ's Divine Will reigns in the souls of men for a prolonged period in human history, symbolized by the expression "one thousand years."
+ All creation rejoices in God's gifts of universal peace, holiness and justice. It is the new Pentecost, the Triumph of the Immaculate Heart and the Eucharistic Reign of Jesus.
+ Shortly before the end of the Era of Peace, Satan is released. He assembles all the pagan nations to wage war on God's holy city.
+ The pagan nations surround the holy city, "then the last anger of God shall come upon the nations, and shall utterly destroy them" and the world shall go down in a great conflagration.
+ Christ returns, and with the breath of his mouth defeats Gog, Magog and Satan who are thrown into the fiery lake for all eternity. There ensues the resurrection and the General Judgment of the living and the dead, in which the righteous will be raised to eternal happiness and the unrighteous delivered to everlasting punishments.
+ God renews the universe: the heavens are folded up, God creates New heavens and a New Earth, and men are

transformed "into the similitude of angels" and rejoice in God's beatific vision for all eternity.

8.2   New Jerusalem, New Heavens and New Earth

After God defeats Satan and casts him down to the fiery lake, , there will take place the Resurrection of all the dead and the General Judgment. Then the New Jerusalem will "come down out of heaven from God, prepared as a bride adorned for her husband."[215] The depictions of Revelation 21 and 22 present the New Jerusalem as a luminous and unblemished city whose gates never close. Like Mary and the Apostles who behold God face-toface, those who enter this heavenly city partake of the beatific vision. It is in this eternal and perfected kingdom which Christ hands over to his Father after destroying every ruler and authority that the Lord's elect reign with him. Unlike the New Jerusalem, the "New Heavens and New Earth" is not just the planet earth, but the entire cosmos with all its galactic systems transformed by God for mankind's new modality of existence.

The renewed universe will reflect the countenance of the Trinity in its omnipresence and omniscience. St. Thomas Aquinas, in his work entitled *Quaestiones Disputatae*, comments on the earth's final transformation and on the duration of its composite substances:

> The sense of the passages quoted (2 Pt 3:10: "The heavens shall pass away"; Lk 21:33: "Heaven and earth will pass away") is not that the substance of the world will perish, but that its outward appearance will vanish according to the Apostle (1 Cor 7:31).[216]

---

[215] Rev. 21:2.

[216] St. Thomas Aquinas, *Quaestiones Disputatae*, (Roma, Italy: Editrice Marietti, 1965), Vol. II De Potentia, Q. 5, Art. 5, p. 140.

The breathtaking reflections of God in nature will become sublimated, perfected and deified in God to conform to his deified children. Mountains, valleys, plains, fields, meadows, rivers and seas will assume new forms for the glorified sons and daughters of God, such that their enigmatic "passing away" is correctly understood not as an annihilation but as a transformation. As the dwelling place for the Incarnate Son of God, of the Redeemer not only of man but of the entire universe, the earth will remain in substance and will be received by him in all its beauty. Since God sent his only Son to the world not to condemn but to save it, it follows that He will indeed save it.

As for the sons and daughters of God who possess the earth, they will be the same persons they were in their pilgrim state and yet different—with the same bodies and souls they had in history, yet different. Like Jesus, they will possess material bodies that have been "glorified" to conform to their new modality of existence. Since they retain their humanity, their senses will remain. They will be able to see, hear, taste, smell and feel without being confined to time or space, but in a "beatific mode" of existence, "for the kingdom of God is not a matter of food and drink, but of righteousness, peace and joy in the Holy Spirit."[217] Their "spiritual bodies," comprised of glorified bodies and glorified souls, will continue to increase in power. These powers of soul and body may be called paranormal, telepathic, clairvoyant, cognitive, retrocognitive, psycho-kinetic, projective and communicative. They will be impassible and immortal, resplendent, beautiful and radiant with the glorious light of their souls illuminating their bodies. They will compenetrate other bodies of matter at will; and they will be agile, so as to move easily from one place to another, perhaps from one planet to another with the speed of thought.

In contrast to former notions of heaven as a static place of eternal rest and immobility, contemporary theology admits growth and progress in perfection, happiness and beauty throughout eternity. While the beatific vision infuses within glorified man in a single instant the complete knowledge of God, the explication of that knowledge deepens throughout

---

[217] Rom 14:17.

eternity. In heaven mobility is admitted on the more human level, for the ongoing human perfections of glorified man. Surely a God who carefully molded the human traits in his only begotten Son, to be assumed and sanctified for man's Redemption, would adopt this standard for the mankind he redeemed. For this reason all bodies rejoined to their souls will continue to admit growth in perfection, even in their perfected state.

At the center of the New Heavens and New Earth is the New Jerusalem, a place one may imagine filled with God's eternal light, singing, rejoicing, in perfect communion with the saints in heaven, who may visit or dwell therein. One of the most fascinating passages in Scripture is St. John's description of the New Jerusalem:

> The earth and the sky fled from his presence
> and there was no place for them... Then I saw a
> new heaven and a new earth. The former heaven
> and the former earth had passed away, and the
> sea was no more. I also saw the holy city, a new
> Jerusalem, coming down out of heaven as a bride
> adorned for her husband. I heard a loud voice
> from the throne saying, *"Behold, God's dwelling*
> *is with the human race..."* I saw no temple in the
> city, for its temple is the Lord God almighty
> and the Lamb... the river of life-giving water
> sparkling like crystal, flowing from the throne
> of God and of the Lamb down the middle of its
> street... Nothing accursed will be found there
> anymore. The throne of God and of the Lamb
> will be in it, and his servants shall worship him.
> Night will be no more, nor will they need light
> from lamp or the sun.[218]

Interpreters have been impressed by this imagery of the New Jerusalem. W.M. Smith stated that since it is seen coming down from heaven, the New Jerusalem *"is not to be identified with heaven... rather it is part of the new heaven and new earth."*[219] Interestingly, the Old Jerusalem

---

[218] Rev 20:11; 21:1-3. 22; 22:1-3.

[219] W.M. Smith, *The Biblical Doctrine of Heaven,* (Chicago: Moody Press, 1968).

was the religious center of Israel, the city over which the redeemer wept and centered on the temple area where he prayed and taught. If the New Jerusalem merits the name it bears, it must then signify to some degree the religious center where God will be with his people in a very special and eternal way; where there will be no man-made temple but a temple which *"is the Lord God almighty and the Lamb."*[220]

Unlike a static chamber where the dead rest in immobility, heaven emerges in light of recent scholarship as a dynamic dimension with two extensions: the New Jerusalem that stands at the center of the entire cosmos, and the New Heavens and New Earth. These two extensions of God's abode—where his supreme glory and presence are manifest—are created by God for the glory and splendor of creation. The separations of earth and sky, matter and spirit coalesce to form the New Heavens and New Earth, with Christ Jesus as its center. The sublime fusion of the spiritual and material orders welcomes the sons of God into its endless regions of uninterrupted and eternal communion with the angels and their Creator.

As humanity journeys into the third Christian millennium, the message of God's prophets reminds us of the glory that awaits us. Their messages dispose and prepare us for the approaching days of Antichrist and, more importantly, they direct our attention to the glories of the New Heavens and New Earth that await us. Many early Church Fathers, Writers, Doctors and mystics have foreseen the times in which we live, and stoutly invite us to meet them with unlimited trust in God's infinite mercy. I join them in welcoming you to trust where there is no hope, to believe where there is no faith, and to pray when all else have ceased to pray. May this work increase your knowledge of the Last Things, and may the knowledge you derive from it dispose you to a more intimate and loving union with God.

Fiat!

---

[220] Rev 21:22.

BIBLIOGRAPHY

Justin, Martyr, Saint. "Dialogue with Trypho," in v. 6, *Writings of Saint Justin Martyr,* a new translation by Thomas B. Falls, in *The Fathers of the Church* Series. New York, Christian Heritage, 1949

Bequillon, Bertina, Saint, in vol. 1 of Curicque, J.-M., Abbott, *Voix prophétiques; ou, Signes, apparitions et prédictions modernes touchant les grands événements de la Chrétienté au XIXe siècle et vers l'approche de la fin des temps,* 5 éd., rev., cor. et augm, Paris, V. Palmé; Bruxelles, A. Vromant [etc.] 1872, 2 vols.

Frela, A. "Electromagnetic Swords in Alaska," in the Russian newspaper *The Limit of Impossibility* 20, 1999 (Published in Russian; reference translated by Rev. Iannuzzi).

Kondrashov, A., "21st Century Death Rays," in the Russian newspaper *Arguments and Factors* 24, 2000 (published in Russian; reference translated by Rev. Iannuzzi).

Orchard, Bernard, Dom. *Catholic Commentary on Holy Scripture.* Ed. by Dom Bernard Orchard et al., with a foreword by the Cardinal Archbishop of Westminster. London, Edinburgh, Paris, Melbourne, Toronto, and New York: Thomas Nelson and Sons, 1951.

Acta Apostolicae Sedis 73, Vatican City, Europe, 1981.

Irenaeus of Lyons, Saint. "Adversus Haereses," in *The Fathers of the Church.* New York: CIMA Publishing Co., 1947.

Albert J. Hebert, Wonders and Response, P.O. Box 309, Paulina, LA,1988.

Albert J. Herbert, S.M., Signs, Wonders and Response, (LA: 1988).

Solovyov, Vladimir Sergeyevich. *War, progress, and the end of history, including a short story of the Anti-Christ. Three discussions by Vladimir Soloviev,* translated from the Russian by Alexander Bakshy, with a biographical notice by Dr. Hagberg Wright. London: publ. for the Universiy of London Press, Ltd., by Hodder & Stoughton, 1915.

Aristide Serra, "Lo Spirito Santo e Maria in Lc 1,35. Antico e Nuovo Testamento a confronto," in *Parola, Spirito e Vita*, 2 (Jul-Dec. 1998), pp. 119-140. *Collana Lo Spirito Santo.* Bologna: Centro editoriale dehoniano.

B.Y. Tichoplav-T.S. Tichoplav, The Great Passage, VES [Fizika very] St. Petersburg [Vera] Russia 2002 (published in Russian; reference translated by Rev. Iannuzzi).

Bellarmini, *Opera Omnia, Disputationem Roberti Bellarmini. De Controversiis, Christianae Fidei*, Tomus Primus, Liber Tertius, *De Summo Pontefice.* Caput II, *Antichristum certum quemdam hominem futurum*, Liber Tertius. 1577.

Bellarmino, Roberto Francesco Romolo, Saint. *De Romano Pontefice.* Neapoli: apud Josephum Giuliano, 1856.

Bellarmino, Roberto Francesco Romolo, Saint. *Disputationes de controversiis christianae fidei adversus hujus temporis haereticos.* Venetiis, 1721-28.

Bellarmino, Roberto Francesco Romolo, Saint. *Power of the Pope in temporal affairs, against William Barclay; Cologne, 1610.* Translated and edited by George Albert Moore. Chevy Chase, Md.: Country Dollar Press, 1950.

Bélanger, Blessed Dina. *The Autobiography of Blessed Dina Bélanger*, translated by Mary St. Stephen. R.J.M., 1997.

Pius IX, Pope, Blessed."19th Century," in Yves Dupont, *Catholic Prophecy, The Coming Chastisement.* Rockford, IL: Tan Books and Pub., 1973.

Petrisko, Thomas W. *Call of the Ages.* Santa Barbara, CA: Queenship Publishing Co., 1995.

Catholic Church. *Catechism of the Catholic Church.* Vatican City: Libreria Editrice Vaticana, 1994, distr. by St. Paul Books & Media, 1994, art. 1258.

Felix, Minucius. *Commodianus. Instructions in Favor of Christian Discipline Against the Gods of the Heathens.* Whitefish, Montana: Kessinger Publishing, 2004.

The Writings Of Tertullian III With The Extant Works Of Victorinus And Commodianus, part of the *Ante Nicene Christian Library Translations Of The Writings Of The Fathers Down To Ad 325.* Ed. by Alexander Roberts and James Donaldson. Whitefish, Montana: Kessinger Publishing, 2004.

Jerome, Saint. *S. Hieronymi Presbyteri. Opera*, Pars I [v.] 5 "Commentariorum in Danielem Libri III (IV)," in *Corpus Christianorum, Series Latina*, vols. 72-80. Turnholti: Typographi Brepol, Editores Pontifici, 1964. Turnholti: Brepols, 1958.

John Damascene, Saint. "De Fide Orthodoxa," in vol. 37 of *The Fathers of the Church*. Translated by Frederick H. Chase, Jr., New York: The Fathers of the Church, Inc. 1958.

Piux XI, Pope. *"Divini Redemptoris." Encyclical Letter on Atheistic Communism*. Washington, D.C., National Catholic Welfare Conference, 1937.

http://www.papalencyclicals.net/Pius11/ P11DIVIN.HTM

St. Ephraem, in *The Sunday sermons of the great Fathers*. Translated and edited by M. F. Toal. New ed. San Francisco: Ignatius Press, 2000. 4 vols.

The Sunday sermons of the great Fathers. Translated and edited by M. F. Toal. Chicago: Regnery, 1958.

Meklenburg, E. "Psycho-Weapons and the Military Strategy of the 21st Century," in the Russian newspaper *The Terminator* 1996 (published in Russian; reference translated by Rev. Iannuzzi).

Balthasar, Hans Urs von. *Studies in Theological Styles: Lay styles*, vol. 3 of *The glory of the Lord : A Theological Aesthetics*. Translated by Erasmo Leiva-Merikakis; edited by Joseph Fessio and John Riches. San Francisco: Ignatius Press; New York: Crossroad Publications, 1983-1991. 7 vols.

Hippolytus. *Extant Works and Fragments, Dogmatical and Historical,* Part II, "Treatise on Christ and Antichrist," in vol. 5 of *The Ante-Nicene Fathers: Translations of the writings of the fathers down to A.D. 325*. Edited by Alexander Roberts and James Donaldson. Edinburgh: T. & T. Clark; Grand Rapids, Mich.: W.B. Eerdmanns, 1989-1994. 10 vols..

http://www.crystalinks.com/haarp.htm

Ianizkiy, I. N. *Physics and Religion*. Moscow: Russian Physics Community Edition, The Advantage of Society Pub House, 1995 (published in Russian; reference translated by Rev. Iannuzzi).

Michael Brown, The Bridge to Heaven, Spirit Daily Pub., 1993.

Amorth, Father Gabriel. Article in *Inside the Vatican* (Jan. 1994), New Hope, KY: Urbi et Orbi Communications, 1993.

New American Bible. St. Joseph Edition. New York: Catholic Book Pub. Co, 1991.

Auer, Johann and Joseph Ratzinger. "Dogmatic Theology" in *Eschatology* 9, Catholic University of America Press, Washington DC, (1988).

Benedict XVI, Pope (Joseph Ratzinger). *Eschatology, Death and Eternal Life.* Translated by Michael Waldstein; translation edited by Aidan Nichols. Washington, D.C.: Catholic University of America Press, c1988.

Lactantius. *The Divine Institutes,* in vol. 7 of *The Ante-Nicene Fathers.* Peabody, MA: Henrickson Pub., 1995.

Leopoldo Mandic, http://personal.lig.bellsouth.net/l/a/lasereye/may02.html.

Bridget of Sweden, Saint. *Revelations of St. Bridget on the Life and Passion of Our Lord and the Life of His Blessed Mother.* Rockford, Ill.: Tan Books & Publishers, June 1984.

Bridget of Sweden, Saint. *St. Bridget's Revelations to the Popes: an edition of the so-called Tractatus de summis pontificibus.* Edited by Arne Johansson. Lund, Sweden: Lund University Press, 1997.

Bridget, of Sweden, Saint. *The revelations of St. Birgitta of Sweden.* Translated by Denis Searby; introductions and notes by Bridget Morris. New York : Oxford University Press, 2005.

Willey, David. "Cardinal: Antichrist is Vegetarian," *London Times,* Friday, March 10, 2000; cf. also BBC News, article of March 6, 2000, http://news.bbc.co.uk/1/hi/world/europe/668048.stm.

Piccarreta, Luisa. *Pro-manoscritti.* Milan: Associazione del Divin Volere, Casa Editrice di Francesco Gamba, 1977

Vatican Council II, *Lumen Gentium.* Northport, NY: Costello Pub. Co. rev. ed., 1988

Maria Esperanza, Volume 15-n.2 Featured Article, from www.sign.org.

Naju, Korea, Message of Nov. 26, 1989. http://www.marystouch.com/truth/status.htm.

L'Osservatore Romano, Vatican City, Europe. Editorial and Management Offices of the Vatican. August, 2000.

Our Lady of the Rosary Library Prospect, KY Website: www.olrl.org/lives/

John Paul II, Pole (Karolus Vojtyla). *The Theology of the Body.* With a foreword by John S. Grabowski.Boston: Pauline Books & Media, 1997.

Pope Pius XII. "Divino Afflante Spiritu," 33-34, http://www.vatican.va/holy_father/pius_xii/encyclicals/index.htm:

Septuagint Bible. Septuaginta; id est, Vetus Testamentum Graece iuxta LXX interpretes. Edidit Alfred Rahlfs. Stuttgart: Württembergische Bibelanstalt: 1971, c1935. 2 vols.

Otto, Helen Tzima. *When Heaven broke the seals and opened the scrolls.* Rockhill, So. Carolina:Verenikia Press, 1998.

Augustine of Hippo. "City of God," in *The Ante-Nicene fathers. Translations of the writings of the fathers down to A.D. 325.* The Rev. Alexander Roberts and James Donaldson, editors. Edinburgh: T. & T. Clark ; Grand Rapids, Mich.: W.B. Eerdmanns, 1989-1994. 10 vols.

Jørgensen, Johannes. *Saint Bridget of Sweden.* Translated from the Danish by Ingeborg Lund.

London, New York: Longmans, Green, 1954. 2 vols.

Clement of Rome, Saint. *The Clementine Homilies*, Homily II, "First the Worse, Then the Better," in vol. 17 of *The Ante-Nicene Christian Library: Translations of the writings of the fathers down to A.D. 325.* Edited by Alexander Roberts and James Donaldson. Edinburgh, T. and T. Clark, 1867-73. 24 vols.

Elizabeth Canori-Mora, Saint, in *The Christian trumpet, or, Previsions and predictions about impending general calamities, the universal triumph of the church, the coming of Anti-Christ, the last judgement, and the end of the world.* Compiled by Father Pellegrino. Boston: P. Donahoe, 1873.

Hildegard, Saint. "Divinum Operorum," in Yves Dupont, *Catholic Prophecy, The Coming Chastisement.* Rockford, IL: Tan Books and Pub., 1973.

Irenaeus of Lyons, Saint. "Adversus Haereses," in *The Fathers of the Church.* New York: CIMA Publishing Co., 1947.

Irenaeus of Lyons, Saint. "Fragments," in vol. 5 of *The Ante-Nicene Christian library; translations of the writings of the Fathers down to A.D. 325.* Edited by Alexander Roberts and James Donaldson. Edinburgh, T. and T. Clark, 1867-73. 24 vols.

John Vianney, Saint, in *The Christian trumpet, or, Previsions and predictions about impending general calamities, the universal triumph of the church, the coming of Anti-Christ, the last judgement, and the end of the world.* Compiled by Father Pellegrino. Boston: Thos B. Noonan & Co., Boston, 1873.

Martyr, Justin. "Dialogue with Trypho," *The Fathers of the Church*, Christian Heritage, New York 1948.

De Montfort, Louis-Marie Grignion, Saint. *True Devotion to Mary.* Rockford, Ill.: TAN Books, 1985.

Kowalska, Maria Faustina, Saint. *Diary, Divine Mercy in My Soul.* Stockbridge, Mass.: Marians of the Immaculate Conception, 2000.

Bellarmine, Robert, Saint, in Birch, Desmond. *Trial, Tribulation & Triumph: Before, During and after Antichrist.* Santa Barbara, Calif.: Queenship Publishing, 1997.

Aquinas, Thomas, Saint. *Quaestiones Disputatae,* vol. II, "De Potentia." Rome: Editrice Marietti, 1965.

Vincent Ferrer, Saint. "Sermo de Sancto Domenico," *Sermones de Sanctis,* Reeves, Antwerp, 1573, in O'Connor, Edward D., Father. *Marian Apparitions Today: Why So Many?* Santa Barbara, Calif.: Queenship Publ. Co. 1997.

Vincent Ferrer, Saint. "Mirabile Opusculum de Fine Mundi," 1483, no place of publication, in Reeves, Marjorie. *The influence of prophecy in the later Middle Ages; a study in Joachimism.*Oxford: Clarendon, 1969.

Aquinas, Thomas, Saint. *Summa Theologica.* New York: Benzinger Bros., 1947.

Tertullian, "The Soul's Testimony," in *The Ante-Nicene Fathers,* Henrickson Pub., Peabody, MA, 1995.

Tertullian. "Adversus Marcion," *The Ante-Nicene Fathers,* Henrickson Pub., Peabody, MA, 1995.

Tertullian. "Apology of Christianity," *The Ante-Nicene Fathers,* Henrickson Pub., Peabody, MA, 1995.

Augustine of Hippo, Saint. "On the Psalms," in *The Ancient Christian Writers.* Edited by Johannes Quasten and Jopseh C. Plumpe. Westiminster, Maryland: The Newman Press, c1946-. 40 vols.

Mary Catherine, Sister, ed.. *Angel of the judgment: A life of Vincent Ferrer.* Notre Dame, Ind.: Ave Maria Press, 1954.

Cyril, Saint, "The Catechetical Lectures of S. Cyril, Archbishop of Jerusalem." Translated by R. W. Church. in vol. 2 of *A Library of the Fathers of the Holy Catholic Church.* Oxford: John Henry Parker; London : F. and J. Rivington, 1838.

Emmerich, Anne Catherine. *The Life of Jesus Christ and Biblical Revelations.* Edited by the Very Reverend Carl E. Schmoger. Rockford, Ill.: Tan Books and Publishers, Inc., 2003. 4 vols.

Iannuzzi, Joseph, Rev. *The Splendor of Creation.* McKees Rocks, Penn.: Andrew's Productions, 2004.

Catholic Church. *The Teaching of the Catholic Church: A Summary of Catholic Doctrine.* London: Burns Oates & Washbourne, 1952.

Petrisko, Thomas W. *The Fatima Prophecies.* Steubenville Pie, Penn.: St. Andrew's Productions, 1998.

Herbert, Albert J. *The three days' darkness: Prophecies of saints and seers.* A.J. Hebert, 1986.

V.J. Tihoplav – T.S. Tihoplav, The Great Journey, VES Publications, St. Petersburg, Russia 2002 (published in Russian; reference translated by Rev. Iannuzzi).

Cabrera de Armida, Venerable Concepciòn. *To My Priests [A Mis Sacerdotes].* Cleveland, OH: Archangel Crusade of Love, 1996.

Vincent Ferrer, Saint. "The Prophets and Our Times, in Yves Dupont, *Catholic Prophecy, The Coming Chastisement.* Rockford, IL: Tan Books and Pub., 1973.

Smith, W. M. *The Biblical Doctrine of Heaven.* Chicago: Moody Press, 1968.

www.kurescek.info/sacred-heart-the-nine-first-fridaydevotion. html. Imprimatur: E. Morrogh Bernard. Vic. Gen., Westmonasterii, 1954.

Holzhauser, Bartholomaeus. *Interprétation de l'Apocalypse, renfermant l'histoire des sept ages de l'église catholique. Par le vénérable serviteur de Dieu, ouvrage traduit du latin e continue par le chanoine de Wuilleret ...* Paris, L. Vives, 1856.

Cyril, Saint, "Instructions of S. Cyril, Archbishop of Jerusalem." Translated by R. W. Church in *A Library of the Fathers of the Holy Catholic Church.* Oxford: John Henry Parker; London : F. and J. Rivington, 1838.

Chrysostom, Saint, "commentary On II Thess.," in *Corpus Christianorum, Series Latina,*

De Montfort, Louis-Marie Grignion, Saint, et al. *Jesus Living in Mary: Handbook of the Spirituality of St. Louis de Montfort.* Bayshore, NY: Montfort Publications, Bayshore, NY, 1995.

McGinn, Bernard. *Antichrist: Two Thousand Years of the Human Fascination with Evil.* San Francisco: Harper, c1994.

ABOUT THE AUTHOR

Rev. Joseph L. Iannuzzi is a theologian and doctoral alumnus of the Gregorian Pontifical University. As a former freestyle and greco-roman wrestler, Fr. Iannuzzi pursued postgraduate studies in biology, philosophy and theology at seven universities in North America and in Europe. He has translated six theological works from Italian to English, and he was an associate exorcist of Fr. Gabriel Amorth, the exorcist of Rome.

Fr. Joseph is member of the missionary religious community located in the Diocese of Marquette, MI that enjoys the ecclesiastical approval of his local bishop and the added endorsements of two bishops of the Detroit Diocese. As an international association that promotes the Church's mystical tradition, the missionary community provides solo-wilderness retreats at the CCL (Companions of Christ the Lamb) spiritual center that spans well over 1,000 acres of verdure in the village of Paradise, MI. Those interested in making solo-wilderness retreats to deepen their union with God's Divine Will may contact Fr. Joseph at soulofjesus@juno.com.

Fr. Joseph is presently completing a dissertation on the writings and doctrines of the Servant of God Luisa Piccarreta at the Pontifical University of Rome. He is the author of five books on mystical and dogmatic theology, the initiator of international Divine Will communities and instructor on the proper theological presentation of the mystical gift of *Living in God's Divine Will.*

ADDITIONAL RESOURCES BY REV. IANNUZZI!

The Splendor of Creation

In this groundbreaking book, theologian Fr. Joseph Iannuzzi discusses a period of time in the not-to-distant future that many Christians eagerly await–the coming era of peace known as the Millennium. Written from a scholarly, theological perspective, the Splendor of Creation is readable, well documented, and highly informative. The figurative thousand-year era of peace that is foretold in the twentieth chapter of St. John's book of Revelation is the subject of this work. $ 19.95 + $3.95 s/h

Proper Catholic Perspectives

On the Teachings of Luisa Piccarreta

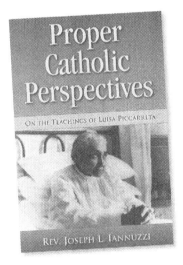

Fr. Joseph Iannuzzi, an expert on the writings of Luisa Piccarreta, now brings to us even greater clarity on these writings as *Proper Catholic Perspectives of* is a treasure of wisdom that readers will find priceless in their desire to totally embrace the theology of the Divine Will. The Cause of Beatification of the Servant of God Luisa Piccarreta was opened in Rome in 1994 and is still underway at this time.

$9.95 + $3.95 s/h

 To Order, call (412) 787-9735 or visit www.SaintAndrew.com

ANOTHER GREAT TITLE BY REV. IANNUZZI!

'This book is a ground breaking masterpiece. It is the most authoritative book ever written on the subject. Iannuzzi's bold text clearly documents how scripture and church teachings define and foretell the coming triumph of God's Kingdom on earth.'

—Dr. Thomas Petrisko,
Author, Call of The Ages

This is the most authoritative resource on the Millennium and End Times. If you have ever read similar books by Hal Lindsey, Ted Flynn, Grant Jeffrey, Tom Petrisko, Rev. Vincent Micelli, or even yours truly, then you will benefit greatly from this book. It is a gift of the Holy Spirit, who will speak to your heart as you read it.

—Bud Macfarlane, Jr., MI,
Author, Pierced By A Sword

The Triumph of God's Kingdom in the Millennium and End Times
A PROPER BELIEF FROM THE TRUTH IN SCRIPTURE AND CHURCH TEACHINGS

The most authoritative book ever written on the Millennium and End Times. It provides solid answers on one of the most confusing but important topics today. This book removes fear and conclusively shows the error of the "Pre Trib Rapture", and demonstrates the reality of God's Kingdom on earth where Christ will reign but not in the flesh. Based solely on Scripture, Fathers and Doctors of the Church, and approved Church teachings, this book is a one-of-a kind treasure. $ 14.95 + $3.95 s/h

To Order
Call 1-412-787-9735

CPSIA information can be obtained
at www.ICGtesting.com
Printed in the USA
LVHW101135311022
731989LV00001B/27